Bleeding in the Pews

Delivered From Rejection, Molestation, Rape, Shame & Fear

Corine H. Stone

Copyright © 2014 Corine H. Stone

All rights reserved.

ISBN: 1936867125
ISBN-13: 978-1936867127

Bleeding in the Pews

Copyright ©2014 Corine H. Stone

Published by Destiny House Publishing, LLC

ISBN-13: 978-1936867127
ISBN-10: 1936867125

Unless otherwise stated, all scripture quotations are from the Holy Bible, King James Version. Scripture references that do not have the Bible version noted are the author's paraphrase.

Editing: Cover design and Publication

Layout: Destiny House Publishing, LLC

Artwork: Canstock Photo

ALL RIGHTS RESERVED

All rights reserved under International Copyright law.

No part of this book may be reproduced or transmitted in any form or by any means: electronic, mechanical, including photocopying and recording, or by any information storage and retrieval system, without permission in writing from the publisher.

Printed in the United States of America

For information:

Destiny House Publishing, LLC

www.destinyhousepublishing.com

Email: inquiry@destinyhousepublishing.com

P.O. Box 19774

Detroit, MI 48219

888-890 9455

Prayer for Those Who Read This Book:

Father in the name of Jesus, I give You all the Honor, Glory and Praise because it is due You. Thank You right now for all You are to me. I thank you for the journey you put me on at birth. Thank you, Father for choosing me to live the life I have lived. I thank You for every trial, pain, challenge you have bought me through because it prepared me for such a time as this. You are the only true and living God; I reverence You, God in Jesus name.

Now Father, I lift up every individual who will read this book. I pray for them now. I ask that as they read the book to give them clarity of thought and mind. Give them understanding about the horrors of sexual, emotional and physical abuse. Help them to be compassionate and caring about individuals who have suffered, are suffering and will be suffering at the hands of individuals, known and unknown, who have or will hurt them. Father, in the name of Jesus I ask for Your knowledge, wisdom, and revelation to be released to those who will read the following pages.

Father God, I ask you to bless, touch and heal those who will read this book who have been victimized by sexual, emotional and physical abuse. Heal their wounds; stop the blood that runs from their wounds. I bind all the horrible memories that assault them on a daily basis. I ask You Lord to heal their heart of unforgiveness, bitterness and hatred. Father, move on their behalf now. God, I bind all their feelings of rejection, pain, hurt, anger and disappointments. I loose a heavenly host of angels in their lives. I loose the blood of Jesus over their lives. I loose healing in their relationships. For You said in You word that, **"And I will give you the keys of the kingdom of heaven, and whatever you bind on earth will be bound in heaven, and whatever you loose on earth will be loosed in heaven" (Matthew 16:19).** Father God, release healing in their inner parts, Lord. Cause them to feel and experience what is good and right in their relationships.

I speak life to you and please know that healing is available to you right now. It's in your hands. I love you.

Corine H. Stone

DEDICATION

To my Lord and Savior Jesus Christ Who called, sent, and set me in the Body of Christ as an apostle and placed a mantle of deliverance on my life.

To my dear, darling, late husband, Pastor Schuyler V. Stone. For the promises you kept and for the love that remains.

To my children: Victor, Freda, and Ronneisha; and grandchildren: Vic II, TeKeia, Jyreh Corine, and Sammie, Jr. who have shown me unconditional love. You have shown me love continuously as God took me through my healing process. I thank God for each of you because you have been my reasons to live when the enemy desired to take my life. Thank you for always being there for me. Thank you for not holding anything against me. Without you, there would be no book. I love you.

To Schuyler's children, the Family Stone: Marshon, Robynee, Shannon, Schuyler II, Shara and Tyler.

To my parents, Luther and Elzina Williams for being the vessels God chose to use to bring me forth and for giving me the best that you could. I love you.

To my maternal grandmother, the late Annie Gammon Gilbert, for loving me to life.

To my siblings: Shirley Williams (deceased), Luther Williams, Pearl Anna Stevenson (deceased), Sherry Evans, Stanley Williams, Dinial

Williams, Paul Williams, and Darryl Williams; I love you all dearly. Thank you for always being here for me.

To my aunts: Annie Mae McClinton, MV Buchanan, and Wyvonia Elizabeth Davis, and my uncles: Jonathan Gammon, Eddie Gammon, and Zack Gammon for always being a bridge of love.

To my Love & Deliverance International Ministries' family where I serve as the senior pastor & overseer, I appreciate the undying love and support you have given me. You are simply the greatest and I love each of you. To some very special supporters: Phyllis, Devonne, Loretta, Robert H., Nickole, Willie Mae, Jackie, Robert M. and Phylicia, thank for your love and support down through the years as I obeyed the call of God on my life. You are a constant reminder of how much God loves me.

To my spiritual sons and daughters throughout this nation and others who have put a demand on the anointing on my life because they saw the value and thrived. Thank you for your pursuit of what God placed in me. I love you.

To Juanita Edwards-Thomas, Addie Cooper and Betty McCullough my dearest friends. Thank you for your friendship and love.

To all my enemies that discouraged, spoke negative words, and made accusations against me. Thank you for misunderstanding me. I forgive you and I love you. All you have done or said against me has helped launch me into my destiny. Thank you and God bless you.

CONTENTS

	Acknowledgments	9
	Introduction	23
1	Born for Purpose	29
2	My Divine Call From God	35
3	Spirit of Rejection Enters	41
4	The Molestation Begins	51
5	Raped Twice-Two Men-In The Same Day	63
6	Blanketed in the Spirit of Shame	75
7	Engulfed and Bound By Fear	85
8	Searching for Love in All the Wrong Places	93
9	My Journey to Deliverance and Healing	143
10	Conclusion	175
11	Appendix	181
	Dr. Phil's Child Sexual Abuse Warning Signs	183
	Adult Symptoms Child Sexual Abuse	187
	About the Author	189

ACKNOWLEDGMENTS

I would like to honor my spiritual parents and mentors, Apostle Benny & Prophetess Geraldine Dozier for being the godly instruments God used to facilitate my healing and deliverance. I sat under your ministry for nearly twenty-three years before God launched me out to build a ministry for Him. I have a special place in my heart for you because you spoke into my life when I did not know how to love myself. Thank you for loving me unconditionally and adopting me into your family and lives. Outside of God, you are the reason I am walking in my destiny!

I especially want to acknowledge some very dear, close friends and co-laborers in the Gospel: Apostle George and Pastor Grace Akalonu, Apostle Stacy Slaughter, Apostle Sondra Jenkins, Apostle Fred and Prophetess Kathleen Harris, Apostle Francis & Prophet Debra Chinaka, Prophet Cleota and Elder Kevin Porter, Apostles Sam and Irene Enyia and Apostle Kenneth & Prophetess Jacqueline Rhymes

I want to acknowledge my Inner Circle, my great support team, who has stood with me covering, praying and engaging in spiritual warfare against the enemies of my soul who have been sent to destroy me; and assisting me in ministry in any way so that this book would come to fruition.

I want to thank my daughter, Ronneisha Hunt-Jackson for editing this book and praying for me during this process. Thanks for your labor of

Corine H. Stone

love.

I want to thank my brother, Luther Williams and his wife, Mary, for your unselfish love and support when I needed it most.

Foreword

When we experience the pain and sorrow of abuse of any sort, a measure of healing is simply not enough; we must be delivered from the core of our very soul. I am a witness! Today and always, I celebrate my friend, the author Corine Stone, for not just the courage but the wisdom (of God) to offer a source of deliverance to men, women, boys and girls everywhere including those who are "Bleeding in the Pews." People 'perceive' themselves largely through relationships. It's the way God prepared our hearts to receive one another from beginning of time. It is His will that we have care and concern for one another. In this book, you will learn what causes your mind to be swayed to stay in broken abusive relationships, but more importantly how you can take this impartation and be set free by the power of the Almighty God!

Bleeding in the Pews documents Corine's experience with abuse yet it represents a testimony, a journey to wholeness; a journey to deliverance. Although you will walk through this painful time with her, you will find the kind and loving heart of a woman that shares how you, too, can experience deliverance that only Our Father in Heaven can provide. This deliverance will cause you to put a demand on your mind to be changed that you will fulfill your life's purpose and be propelled right into your destiny in spite of the pain from your past. Yes, deliverance is possible and it's yours! Take it from this woman, Apostle Corine Stone. I can truly say, "Look what the Lord has done," when I observe the life of my friend, my comrade, and my sister from then through HIStory. He even delivered her to experience the love of her life... I'll let her share that love story.

Read this work with the love it is intended for you. Let us appreciate the vessel God has used to deliver this message. BE HEALED for your very sake, Amen.

Loving prayers cover you,

Apostle Stacy Slaughter
Gateway Kingdom Ministries, Inc.
Columbus, Ohio

Abuse of any kind may not exactly be an easy subject to openly discuss for the perpetrator or victim. However, once that victim can muster up enough strength to admit, there is a problem and then develop and maintain a successful plan to escape, one can move forward with an inkling of hope. On the flip side, there are women and men who get caught in a vicious cycle and may not have a means of escape or quite frankly are just too afraid to walk away from an abusive situation.

Apostle Corine Stone is a devout Christian who has treaded an unfavorable path and unknowingly participated in a cycle of generational abuse. In this book, she unequivocally describes her own personal struggles with abuse as well as her triumphant victory. For any woman/man who is simply tired of being abused but may not know what steps to take, this book does an excellent job of teaching you how and where to start.

The foundational core of this book stem from Apostle Corine Stone's deep beliefs in the power of God. Apostle Corine Stone is not at all ashamed of what she has endured over the years and she wants to teach others that there is absolutely nothing too hard for God.

Read, meditate, and allow your soul to be fed from the heartfelt writings of *Bleeding in the Pews*.

Minister LaTonia Carr-Williams, Ed.D.
School Psychologist
Chicago, Illinois

Corine H. Stone

Endorsements

There's an "issue of blood" being suffered by the body of Christ that, like the malady of the woman in Matthew 9:20-22, has been ignored, misdiagnosed and/or the subject of spiritual malpractice for many years. Without having researched the precise statistics, we recognize by the Spirit that a high percentage of believers came into relationship with Christ seeking refuge from pain; and for many, that pain was the pain of rape or abuse. The wounds have festered untreated due to shame and in some cases; even perpetuation of the abuse by spiritual leaders unable or unwilling to be the agents of Christ's healing virtue for true deliverance. Jesus tells us in John 8:31-32 that our effectiveness as His disciples is directly tied to the freedom we have achieved through our knowledge of the truth.

We bless God, that He has released His truth on this important issue through the yieldedness and the Spirit-filled transparency of His vessel, Apostle Corine Stone. These words, and the compassion and revelation poured out through them, are an extension of the ministry of love and deliverance in which this woman of God flows with transformational power and impact. To our precious worshipping wounded, read and be blessed! God has seen your tears and heard the cries of your heart. We declare and decree that you shall be made whole from this very hour. Let the healing virtue flow!

Minister Sondra Jenkins
President, Rhema Rain Ministries
Detroit, Michigan

Endorsement for Our Mother

Congratulations to my mother on the completion of your book. I have no ill feelings concerning my upbringing. Our pains, struggles, and love have shaped me into the man I am. I love you Moms.

Victor L. Williams

Words cannot express how much you mean to me. But I truly thank God for giving you to me as a mother. I love you so much and appreciate every sacrifice, pain, punishment, advice, hugs, kisses and support you have ever given me. I pray that one day I will be just as great a mother to my children as you have been to me. I love you to the moon and back. I love you, my beautiful mother. Congratulations on your book!

Freda S. Hunt

To my Mama, I love you with all my heart. You are such an anointed woman of God. You are the best mother I could ever have. You are a great example of a woman who has survived the storms of life. I love you, Mama. Congratulations; can't wait to read your book!

Ronneisha C. Hunt-Jackson

Corine H. Stone

PREFACE

Knocked unconscious by an abusive husband, the woman suddenly awoke and crawled to the bedroom door to see what he was doing. Horrified with tears streaming scathingly down a bloodstained face, she found her husband reading the newspaper as if nothing had happened. She wondered, "How could he beat me and then lay across the bed and continue reading the paper? It was then that she wanted to commit murder. Somewhere down in the middle of her bruised soul, the words, "Don't do it, I have called you to help women in this same situation" flooded her spirit. She remembered thinking, "How, God, how?"

How can a woman in the midst of an abusive relationship escape with her life as well as her children's lives intact? How can a woman fall into the same relationship as her mother? How can she walk in her mother's footsteps after watching her father abuse her mother all her childhood? How can a woman ever love a man who abuses her mentally, emotionally, physically, and sexually? How can she be made whole again?

Respected in her profession, loved by co-workers and church members, but she is hated by the man who professed an undying love to her. How can she stay with a man who not only sleeps with a family member, but a neighbor and a friend? How can she stay even when he has had a child by another woman outside of their marriage? The time to leave is now; there is no better time than now.

To answer these questions, a closer look is required; we must go deeper – to the root problem. The victim or the abused must take that journey; no one can take it for her. If a woman wants to fulfill her purpose and destiny, the journey begins now. The best time to do it is now; there is not a better time than now. If not now, when? The cycle has to be broken.

What then is a cycle? A cycle is circular and will continue for a lifetime or until it is broken. Similarly, abuse operates in a circle. As long as abuse continues in someone's life it will always be a circle of pain, heartbreak and rejection. How can it stop? It begins with a desire to be free; totally free. Freedom can be obtained only if it is sought and fought for without delay. There is a tremendous price to pay to achieve freedom, but it is worth the price paid. God can break circles of abuse!

No matter what your past is, God is a healer and a deliverer. We came to the altar and became saved, but it takes a journey to be "delivered." Deliverance starts with a choice. You must choose this day if you are willing to be delivered and set free. Only you can make this choice. Remember "deliverance" is a choice.

God wants to deliver us from the scars of emotional and sexual abuse plus the spirit of rejection, shame, and fear from our past to move us into His destiny for our lives. It does not matter what your past looks like; God wants to give us a glimpse of our future. Can you see it, "Yes, I can."

I will show you how God can heal you from rejection, sexual molestation, rape, shame, and fear. The cycle of broken relationships can be stopped. If God can deliver me; surely, He will deliver you. The story I will share with you is a story of hurt, pain, disappointment and finally, deliverance. I am the woman in this story.

Corine H. Stone

INTRODUCTION

I know that God allowed me to be born in the midst of segregation where we (Blacks) were kept separate from whites. We actually lived on a plantation in the "black quarters" that was owned by a white, wealthy landowner. I went to an all-Black, one room school. I could only drink out of "colored" water fountains when my mother took me to the nearby town to shop. I remember my mother going to the back of the restaurants to order hamburgers. She was not allowed to enter the front door of the restaurant. I remember my father's boss coming to our house and calling my father "boy". Blacks were treated unequal. Times were hard and very difficult. Blacks suffered gravely during the fifties. My parents were young with two young girls, they did what they could to feed us.

Realizing later as I grew up that there were other key foundational builders who were born that same year as I was, throughout the world, who would implement change in this century, I knew I had been born for purpose. Without a doubt, I am one of them.

Born with a vision and calling in the rural South amid segregation and abject poverty, I now know that it was by God's design that I came forth at the God kind of time. I was born at the right time for an end-time agenda. Due to the assignment on my life, there were spirits released which have fought me since my birth. These spirits were purposely dispatched to derail what had been deposited in my spirit. After being molested and raped, the spirits of rejection, shame, and fear have traveled down my life since I was born. There was a great purpose for the spirits' arrival in my life. They arrived to kill, steal and destroy my purpose.

Before I was formed in my mother's womb, God ordained me to be an Apostle to hurting people in the nations *(Jeremiah 1:5)*. I was called to be an apostle of love and transformation in the many broken lives in families, neighborhoods, cities, and nations. I was also charged with walking in the mantle of *Isaiah 61*. My assignment was to set captives free, change the status quo, challenge traditions of men and help to usher in next move of God in the Body of Christ.

In this very hour, God is raising up a new breed of leaders who have been victims themselves and can recognize and help facilitate healing for those bleeding in the pews. The Psalmist David wrote, **"Send thee help from the sanctuary, and strengthen thee out of Zion" (Psalms 20:2) (KJV).** There is truly "help in the sanctuary" for those bleeding in the pews.

Although many are hurting, they are in the right place to

receive healing right now. God wants to heal those who are wounded, bruised, and battered who are attending numerous churches and yet they are still wounded. He alone is the Healer of our souls. According **to Isaiah 61:1-4**, the Prophet Isaiah declares that, *"The Spirit of the Lord God is upon Me, Because the Lord has anointed Me To preach good tidings to the poor; He has sent Me to heal the brokenhearted, To proclaim liberty to the captives, And the opening of the prison to those who are bound; ² To proclaim the acceptable year of the Lord, And the day of vengeance of our God; To comfort all who mourn, ³ To console those who mourn in Zion, To give them beauty for ashes, The oil of joy for mourning, The garment of praise for the spirit of heaviness; That they may be called trees of righteousness, The planting of the Lord, that He may be glorified. And they shall rebuild the old ruins, They shall raise up the former desolations, And they shall repair the ruined cities, The desolations of many generations."*

God cares about our brokenness and captivity. He sent His Son, Jesus Christ, to set the captives free. Jesus makes the same declaration in the New Testament when He proclaimed that, *"The Spirit of the Lord is upon Me, because He has anointed Me to preach the gospel to the poor; He has sent Me to heal the brokenhearted, to proclaim liberty to the captives and recovery of sight to the blind, to set at liberty those who are oppressed;*

¹⁹ *to proclaim the acceptable year of the L*ORD ***(Luke 4:18-19)."*** When God says something twice, He is establishing something. Luke confirms what the Prophet Isaiah said in Isaiah 61, he confirms Jesus mandate (assignment) here on earth. God loves us so much that He wants us healed from our wounds.

This then is the purpose of this book - to show those of you who are broken that Almighty God sees your issues and He has a way out for you. My goal is to further show others that what He has done for me, He will surely do for you! God healed me, and He can heal you! If God can rescue me from hell, please know the He will do the same for you. If God can use me, surely He will use you. With God all things are possible, but understand this, that we have to come to the road of our impossibility before we can enter God's road of possibility. *"There hath no temptation taken you but such as is common to man: but God is faithful, who will not suffer you to be tempted above that ye are able; but will with the temptation also make a way to escape, that ye may be able to bear it" (1 Corinthians 10:13) (KJV).* God will rescue you from your prisons, and in some cases, even the prisons we have built for ourselves. The church has to shift if it is to be effective in dismantling these prisons.

God wants to change the Body of Christ's methods, but not His message. He is tearing up years of methods, traditions and man-made religions that are not His; and God is raising fearless, end-time warriors (apostles and prophets) who have truly been tried and tested on the battlefield. They will blaze a new path that will usher in what is in God's heart. These unlikely warriors have paid tremendous costs to be used to blaze these paths for God. Many have endured abject poverty, surreal rejection from family, friends, and their denominations, character assassinations, and abuse (sexual, emotional, and physical). As they were birthed and raised by God for this season and this hour, these warriors move at God's command.

The voice we hear is God's. The command we obey is God's. These end time apostles and prophets are not concerned with the voices of the wombs of tradition or religion that nurtured or fed us. The hour is here and the time is now. We must not waver, but move through our Red Seas to get to the place God has called us. The price has been paid in full, the receipt is written in our spirits, so all that is left is to "just do it!"

Corine H. Stone

CHAPTER 1
BORN FOR PURPOSE

I was born in the backdrop of segregation to destitute, young sharecroppers, Luther and Elzina Williams on Tuesday, February 11, 1953 at 10:30 a.m. in a three room "shot-gun" house near a much traveled dirt road in the rural south. I was delivered by my mother's mom, my grandmother, who delivered eight of my mother's nine children. My mother needed a caesarean section for their last child. Delivered by my midwife grandmother, I was the second of nine children born to my parents. In the South a midwife has a very special job because so many people could not afford to go to the hospital. A midwife's job was to "catch" the baby as it emerges from the womb.

From the moment my grandmother caught me, I have been catching hell since that day fighting for a chance to live. Although my birth was pretty ordinary, just living my life has been extraordinary. Being born to poor sharecroppers who never had much of anything and barely enough to feed their growing family was very challenging for me and for my siblings. My parents worked relentlessly to provide the necessities for their growing family during a very trying time when they were on the bottom of the socio-eco heap. I believe that when you are called to be an

Apostle, you will experience much adversity because of the process that you must go through to be developed to get to your calling and destiny. My life began in adversity for purpose. Ironically, I found that my pain had a purpose.

Times were hard for my parents and it was difficult with a small growing family. As a matter of fact, while growing up I only remember having one pair of shoes and two dresses during my childhood. My family ate pinto beans without meat five days a week. We had fried fish that my father caught on Saturdays; and my mother fried the chicken we caught every Sunday. The chickens were our friends. We played with them during the week, but our family would eat them on Sundays. We hungrily ate our friends for dinner. We were so poor we couldn't afford the second "o" in poor; we were "po."

My parents did the best they could for their children, but it was difficult for the young couple as it was for the rest of the community we lived in during that time. Our family was normal then; poor, but normal. Or so I thought. Our worlds would change drastically shortly.

Somehow growing up I sensed somehow that my life was filled with purpose. I came from a family of preachers. My maternal grandfather, Rev. Eddie Gammon, who passed away in 1949 (four years before I was born), was a flat-footed preacher who pastored a Baptist church not far from where I grew up. His wife, my grandmother, Mrs. Annie was a "boot-legged" preacher. A boot-legged preacher is one who preaches without being licensed or ordained. Mrs. Annie preached every time she opened her mouth, whether it was at church, home, field, or anywhere she just happened to be at the time. She had the power to make conviction fall in your spirit and you would start repenting. Her voice carried such authority and she put the fear of God in me as a child. I adored her and would often follow her as she traveled around our town and the surrounding areas. I witnessed her preaching and teaching as she shared her love of God and His word with the communities as she sold her butter and eggs each Saturday.

My grandmother poured a lot of love for church into me as a child and young adult by taking me and my siblings to church every week. Church was a very comforting place for me; it was my refuge. My family were deeply rooted in church and preaching. My grandparents' children were all infused with the gift of preaching and teaching: Uncle Jonathan, my mother, Elzina, Auntie Annie Mae, and her youngest daughter, Wyvonia Elizabeth (we affectionately called her "Aunt Liz") could preach as well as any man.

I came from a family who had a strong Christian faith. My

parents kept their tradition in which they were bought up and raised us in church. They were not the most consistent Christians, but they instilled a fear of God in us. They believed in the tradition of putting their children on the mourner's bench so that our souls would be saved. But my mother also could discern an attack by Satan.

My mother related an event to me later when I was a teen. She told me of the day when she placed me in a basket and tied a rope around my waist that would not allow me to crawl out the basket and into the front yard. It was on a hot August day the same year I was born when I was only a few months old. It was sweltering therefore my mother dressed me only in a diaper. While she washed in the back yard, I played in my basket in the front yard. My mother noticed that I had become rather quiet, so she came around the house and suddenly she saw me playing with a big black snake. When she screamed loudly, the snake crawled away. Snatching me up, she investigated my entire body for snake bites, but thank God, there were none.

Without a shadow of doubt, this snake was sent from the pit of hell, I believe, to kill me. I believe that hell did not want me to come forth into the level in the realm of the spirit. Satan has worked demonic strategies to destroy every essence of my life because he knew who I was destined to be in the spiritual realm.

The enemy of my life knew I was his enemy and would do much damage to his kingdom, so he plotted to take me out, but the Bible says, **"Greater is He who is in me than he that is in the world" (1 John 4:4a).** God never said that the enemy wouldn't attack us or come after us, but what God has placed in us is greater. We can and we will overcome our adversary, the devil, who is the enemy of our lives and souls.

Through the challenges of living my life, I know without a shadow of a doubt that there was a spiritual purpose for being born when I was. I feel that there was a supernatural shift that took place in the spiritual realm when I was born that caused all hell to brake forth in my life. God allowed me to be born me in 1953 along with other strategic warriors who would do damage to Satan's kingdom. There have been specified demons assigned to me since the day of my birth plotting when they could wipe me out, kill me, destroy me and stop be by whatever methods they could.

I like music artist, Kelly Clarkson's line in one of her most popular songs, *'Strong' (What Doesn't Kill You)*, that says, "that which doesn't kill you will make you stronger." Even in my weakest moment, my enemy couldn't kill me, but his efforts to kill, steal and destroy what God placed on the inside of me has helped me to become stronger in God and more focused on the purpose for which I was born. The devil is still the "father of lies". The race is not always given to the swift, neither to the strong, but to the one that endureth to the end. The Bible confirms that, *"The race is not to the swift, nor the battle to the strong, nor bread to the wise, nor riches to men of understanding, nor favor to men of skill; but time and chance happen to them all" (Ecclesiastes 9:11).* The devil could not kill the purpose for which I was born. God gave me the strength to win my race that He had set before me.

As a child I endured things no child should ever undergo or suffer; but I believe that those things I endured were a part of the process God allowed me to go through so that the anointing of an apostle would increase on my life and that I would be an engineer of love and deliverance. God taught me how to love those who didn't love me because it is through God's love that we come to be delivered. My journey began in pain, but ended on the path of love, deliverance, and healing. The Glory belongs to God Who is the Architect of my deliverance!

CHAPTER 2
MY DIVINE CALL FROM GOD

The two figures I believed in as a child were God and Santa Claus. I felt like I had to because they were both associated with love and kindness. My mother instilled in us a deep belief in God by teaching us to pray and go to church. I grew up believing that God lived in the sky and that Santa Claus delivered our Christmas presents by coming through the chimney. I eventually learned (like all children) that my parents were behind my Christmas presents, not Santa Claus. But there were some supernatural encounters I had with God throughout my life that confirmed to me that God was real. It all began with my divine assignment.

The first supernatural experience I had with God was such a profound and mind-blowing encounter. It was at the age of nine when I was on the mourner's bench. During the summer of 1961, our church, Old Jerusalem M.B. Church, was having its annual revival. Children my age and older were told to sit on the mourner's bench during the nightly services so that we could ask God to free our souls from the burning gates of hell. Each night we would get on our knees and pray hard with tears streaming down our cheeks and hollered at a God we could not see. The mothers of the church would stand behind us praying and urging us to keep seeking God. They would be mourning and singing invoking the Lord to save these little sinners. Well one afternoon during the revival my mother sent me to the nearby grocery store.

As I walked to the store, I was praying as the church mothers taught us during revival last night. Suddenly, I heard this booming voice that I had never heard before but I didn't see anyone. The voice said, *"I have called you this day and you will preach My word all over the word."* Chills covered my entire body and I remember shivering. I screamed, "Who are You? Where are You? Preach, who me? Preach, what is that?" It was then that He repeated the same words.

To the tender mind, this sounded so bewildering. Of course, there were no models or examples I could look to for help or hope. Having only seen men preach, I had a hard time envisioning myself preaching or preaching what. Women just sang or ushered in my church, I thought to myself. These words were printed in my spirit and I would never forget them because He always said them again over and over through my childhood and even as I grew into a young adult. God didn't stop the words until I said, "Yes!" I knew it was God and I knew that He was real. It was the God that the church mothers asked us to pray to; it was the God I heard about in my Sunday school classes and church. It was God and in my little soul I was convinced that He was real but He had to be confused about me preaching. I never forgot His voice or words that continue to sleep in my spirit. Throughout my entire life, they never left me.

After this initial encounter with God, all I knew is that God had visited me and had saved my soul as I cried out to Him on the road to the store. Yet, I had a horrible secret that was burning a hole in my soul. It was a secret that caused a conflict in my soul although it allowed me to get the attention I longed to have. At nine years old I felt that I had lived a lifetime already.

The second supernatural experience I had with God was so dramatic that it impacted my life greatly and shifted me to another dimension in understanding the call of God on my life. It was during church service on the first Sunday in January 1977. I had an open vision. By this time, I had been in ministry over five years and was full of zeal and fire for God. God showed me a vision of me covered in blood which would later become the foundation of this book. In the vision, bright red blood ran from the top of my head and covered my entire body. He revealed to me that the vision of the blood flowing over my body on the outside was an indication of the pain that was encased way down deep on the inside of me.

What I didn't know was that God was showing my mother

who was standing nearby a vision of blood flowing from my head and covering my entire body at the very same time. She screamed and said that she saw blood running down my whole body. God further revealed to me that the blood was flowing from my deep, emotional, physical, and psychological wounds which were a result of all the pain I had endured during my life. I could feel the pain in that moment as God dealt with my heart and mind. God showed me the heart of a victor and in that instance He began the process of taking me from victim to victor. This vision was the defining moment that propelled me on my journey of healing.

In the many years since, my third supernatural experience with God that related to my calling and assignment was in March 1996. God showed me a vision and the millions of men, women and children who were *"bleeding in the pews"*. As those who were wounded sat in church services, the preacher would be ministering the word of God; they would be nodding their heads in agreement, but their lives would be in various states of devastation. There was such a great flow of blood issuing from their hearts into the aisles of the churches located around the world. God told me that He was *sending* me as His instrument to heal their wounded hearts and stop the flow of blood in the numerous church pews throughout the world. In that instance, I knew that there were many others just like me whose constant pain was not addressed or checked as I sat in the pews bleeding.

God expanded my understanding and revelation of the countless people in the Body of Christ who come to church weekly, but they are "bleeding in the pews" because they have come wounded, battered, and broken needing help and healing. And yet, many of them don't even realize that they are bleeding or even know that something is wrong or keeping them from healing. Frighteningly, some, like me, have not even realized that they even need healing. Shockingly, this was the state I was in for twenty-nine years of my life after my rapes; I didn't know that I had been traumatized and needed healing. I was *"bleeding in the pews"*. On the other, hand, many know that they are wounded and are seeking healing from their inner traumas. However, even so, many pastors and leaders are ill-equipped to assuage their perfuse bleeding. This is why God has raised a new breed of leaders, like me, who have experienced the same devastating traumas to help facilitate healing in the lives of those *bleeding in the pews.*

Corine H. Stone

CHAPTER 3
THE SPIRIT OF REJECTION ENTERS

The spirit of rejection is debilitating and destructive especially when it enters the very young life of a child. Our question then is what is the spirit of rejection? To understand the spirit of rejection, we must get a clear understanding of *rejection*. Rejection is the feeling or the act of being rejected. According to **Merriam-Webster Dictionary,** *to be rejected is to be cast aside, cast off, and cast away – to be thrown away as having no value."* Rejection causes you to feel unwanted, unloved, useless, worthless and unneeded. It eats away at the epitome of who you are or even at who you are destined to become in life. This is a very dangerous spirit in the life of anyone, especially a child. These are the feelings that hijacked me at a very formative age.

Looking back on my life now, I now realize that the spirit of rejection knocked on the door of my life at a very early age; when I was four years old. My life as I knew it changed forever in 1957 when I lost my five year old sister, a week before her sixth birthday.

My older sister, Shirley, was bright, beautiful, and very brilliant for her age. She had a beautiful caramel-colored complexion like me and she had medium length, thick, curly hair (mine was thin and shorter). Shirley's eyes were bright and brilliant. Her presence and smile would light up any room she entered. She was very special to our parents and especially to me; she was my best friend.

On a cool and crisp morning in mid-November, 1957, my mother made a brief run to our grandmother's house. It was a very short trip and she had asked our next door neighbor, who was our godfather, to keep an eye on my sister and I. Our other siblings: Luther, Jr., three, Pearl, two, Sherry, fourteen months, and Stanley, one month, were over at our godfather's house, but mother had left Shirley and me at home because were in her words, "big girls" at ages five and four. She would be gone less than ten minutes. That's when our world changed forever.

After our Mom left, I told Shirley that I was cold. Shirley and I were acting like little ground-ups; we went outside and picked up small pieces of kindling wood for the coal and wood burning heater. Returning inside, we poured the cold chips into the fold of Shirley's dress, which she quickly placed on the red coals in the heater. Not realizing that the bright red coals would immediately cause her dress to leap into flames upon contact. Her dress caught fire immediately as it touched the coals.

I can still hear her screams now fifty-six years later as she screamed for me to "Run!" I did – going next door for our godfather, I ran as fast as my little legs would take me. Our godfather ran back to the house and recued Shirley from the burning house. He wrapped her smoldering body in a piece-patch quilt and laid her on the front porch. Shirley withered in a horrible agony only she knew.

For as I long as I live, I will forever remember my mother's screams as she ran holding the hem of her dress in her hand as she dashed across the pecan orchard (a shortcut) to the house. "Oh, my God, my children, Lord, please God, please don't let them die!" She screamed over and over. My mother's words sounded like they were coming out in slow motion, like each letter was being stretched by elastic bands and looped together, fashioned like a long rope. Her voice was a vast canon being exploded over the field as she ran like Wilma Rudolph in the Olympics.

Still screaming, my mother was quickly climbing the steep stairs to the porch where she was told that Shirley was badly burned in her mid-section and that her other child was fine. The wretched look on her face tortured my soul as she grabbed my sister and cradled her in her arms. Hot tears (steam was coming out of her tears) streaming down her smooth, caramel skin. My mother glanced over at me and I saw a sigh of relief in her eyes and they turned back to my whimpering sister.

Somehow, one by one, our neighbors rushed to the front porch. My father was at work. People helped my mother down the long flight of stairs as she crutched my sister as Shirley screamed over and over for our mother to put out the fire. Shirley's screams were the last sounds I ever heard her make again. I hear her screams even now like it was yesterday.

My pretty sister with the big smile and soft curly hair would never come up those stairs again. She kept losing consciousness, but when she would come to Shirley screamed for our mother to stop the fire in her belly.

Each of my sister's cries tore my mother to pieces and she became smaller and smaller as she rocked her first-born cradled on her breast as life slipped from her body. In my mind, I just knew my sister would never play with me again. Shirley's whole middle was charcoal black and there was a burnt hole where her belly button used to be. "Oh no, Shirley, don't leave me, please don't leave me!" I cried my little eyes out for her as everyone surrounding our house prayed and prayed for my very, very, best friend and sister.

I still cry for my beautiful sister and only friend. Our family cried and cried; it seemed like forever to my four year old mind.

Shirley lived three weeks and then she died quietly in her sleep a few days before her sixth birthday, which would have been December 16th. My mother told me that the last thing she said to our parents was, "I want some spaghetti." She never got a chance to eat her favorite food. But since my mother told me those words; I now eat "spaghetti" for Shirley and I think of her with each fork full because I somehow feel closer to her spirit each time I eat spaghetti. That's a very special time no one can take from me even now, fifty-seven years later.

I remember standing on the porch that day of the fire watching my mother cry wretchedly over my sister's smoldering and seemingly lifeless body and I knew that I would blame myself for the rest of my life for living. I cried, wishing and hoping I could exchange places with my best friend, my dear beautiful sister who seemed to have all the potential and who seemed to have all of my parents love before the ambulance came. I wanted to be the one laying there wrapped in a blanket. I felt that my Mom and Dad would never forgive me for not changing places with their firstborn child. It never occurred to me how my mother must have felt, or even if she blamed herself. As a child, all I knew then was if I had never said I was cold, she would still be alive.

It was at this point that the spirit of rejection and I started down a devastating path. I began unfailingly trying to please my parents by attempting to make up for the death of their favorite child.

As I recall these horrible memories of the crushing pain I suffered when I lost my sister, my heart feels as if someone is clutching it tight in a fist. My heart pounds rapidly in my chest. I feel a fresh scream in my throat but it is trapped mid-way. I can feel it; I hear it; it's loud and it hurts down in my stomach. I feel the same fire that was in my sister's belly. I whimper because I can't get this ball out of my throat. My eyes roll back in my head as I throw my head back to emit this scream. It's her name in my throat. I am heaving now trying to dislodge the ball of pain lodged in my throat. "Lord, help me; I can't breathe." SHIRLEY. It seems as if elastic tied to each letter, but the pain is calling the letters to come out, come out now. SHIRLEY! SHIRLEY!

I don't remember her funeral. I do know that I have visited her grave many times as an adult and have cried for my big sister who still sleeps in a cold grave instead of me.

How could a four year old know that even greater pain and degradation was right around the corner for her? What could hurt more than losing my sister; better yet, for being the reason my sister lost her life?

The enemy was by my side, hissing in my ear with each question I asked God. He answered me loudly by stealing my innocence ultimately in the process. Unfortunately, he did not stop until he had taken my childhood as well. Piece by piece, the devil hauled bits of me off on his back with each breath I took. All that was left was rejection which would scar my entire life.

    Rejection made me feel worthless, valueless and unwanted after my sister died. I blamed myself for her death and always wished it had been me who had died in the fire. Watching my mother cry day after day burned a hole in my young heart. I didn't know how I could ever make her happy. My mother stopped smiling then and she hardly ever smiled again.

    How does rejection affect the person who is struggling with the effects of it? Rejection affect wounded people in very devastating ways. Robert L. Boldt, writes in *Great Bible Studies*, that, *"Rejection causes emotional wounds, which if not cleansed and released, will grow and fester into spiritual wounds (such as unforgiveness, envy, blaming God, jealousy, etc.). Many people, who have faced rejection and abuse as a child, grow up with unresolved emotional wounds. Those spiritual wounds open us up to evil spirits which love to take advantage of this opportunity to invade us. The goal of the enemy is to get us built up with emotional baggage inside and negative feelings in our hearts against one another, ourselves, and God."* Spiritual wounds open doors and windows so thieves and robbers can come in to our lives and drag off our self-esteem, worth and destiny.

Noticeably, rejection entered my life before I turned five years old and it plagued me for the majority of my life. I came to understand that *"when a person who has a hard time admitting they are wrong, or receiving constructive criticism there is an underlying problem of rejection. How do we know that? Due to the fact that they are basing their identity on who they are and upon their ability to be right about everything. Stubbornness can also be rooted in rejection as well for this same reason. They have to be right, or else they feel worthless... that's because "who they are" (their identity) is based upon them being right."* (Boldt). Over the years during my childhood and youth, I struggled with being right and developed stubbornness as a result of rejection that entered my life during my childhood. **"And to know the love of Christ, which passeth knowledge, that ye might be filled with all the fulness of God" (Ephesians 3:19).** It took many years for me to learn that I was created by a God of love to be loved, accepted, and appreciated. This is a God-given right for our lives.

Rejection then is an agent that Satan uses to destroy us and to prevent us from fulfilling God's purposes for our lives. It causes a person to feel starved for love and acceptance that is already our right. Boldt states that, *"The problem is that when we turn to others or even ourselves for that love and acceptance, we are setting ourselves up for failure and the damage of rejection. Only God can be trusted as the source of our identity."* The enemy used the spirit of rejection and my need for attention, love and approval to open the door other devious doors that would lead down a path of destruction.

Corine H. Stone

CHAPTER 4
THE MOLESTATION BEGINS

For the most part after my sister's death, it seemed to my child's mind that I became invisible to my mother. I didn't understand since I was a child how much she was suffering after losing her little angel. Seriously, I really didn't know how to express my own pain, but I only wanted to take away my mother's pain. No matter how I tried to please or make her happy, I never could take the clouds from her eyes. I cried myself to sleep each night hugging my sister's pillow which would be soggy when I woke up each day. Her pillow gave me solace and comfort in the night and during the day. I wrapped my heart around the memories of our conversations and activities that we did together before she went to heaven to be with God.

But now there is a new thing that I wish I could share with my mother, but I was confused and scared. I wanted to tell her about my secrets, but I was afraid. Well, my secrets were about my father and me.

Shortly after my sister's death, my daddy informed me that I was his favorite girl and that we would spend special time together. My father told me that we would have a very special "secret" that I could not tell anyone, not even my mother. The secret was his explorative hands and fingers in the soft places he seemed to find on or inside my panties. Our time was a time where I felt special and loved by my father. I liked cuddling, hugging, and being carried on his shoulders by my father. I liked our special times together because it was during those times I felt that he belonged only to me. But then they began to take on another nature and this was questionable even for my young age. However, my father convinced me that all daddies shared secrets like this with their very special little girls. I was his special girl. I felt that I finally mattered to someone. By his actions, I felt like my father was not angry at me for Shirley's death. I was special now and we had a secret.

I promised my father that I would never tell anyone about our secret. My father's newfound interest in me overshadowed my mother's grief over my sister's death which left an inevitable void and emptiness in me that would follow me for the rest of my life. Being a five year old little girl, I did not understand my mother's pain; I only knew the constant longing in my soul for love, acceptance, forgiveness and validation. I did not know then that what my father was doing to me was molestation, which is a crime. In the article, **"Child Sexual Abuse,"** child sexual abuse or child molestation is *"a form of child abuse in which an adult or older adolescent uses a child for sexual stimulation. Forms of child sexual abuse include asking or pressuring a child to engage in sexual activities (regardless of the outcome), indecent exposure (of the genitals, female nipples, etc.) to a child with intent to gratify their own sexual desires or to intimidate or groom the child, physical sexual contact with a child, or using a child to produce child pornography. Sexual abuse* *by a family member is a form of incest, and can result in more serious and long-term psychological trauma, especially in the case of parental incest."* A child does not understand the purpose behind abuse nor do they understand sexual gratification. They are not to be blamed for the abuse. It is not their fault or the result of anything they have done that causes the abuse. The American Psychiatric Association finds that, *"children cannot consent to sexual activity with adults, and condemns any such action by an adult. An adult who engages in sexual activity with a child is performing a criminal and immoral act which never can be considered normal or socially acceptable behavior."* Molestation and rape of children are against the laws of the state and heaven. Contrary to popular opinion, children are abused sexually each year at an alarming rate. It is a well-kept secret in most families in this nation and others.

Many times children are lured into molestation by someone familiar to them that they trust. According to *U.S. Bureau of Justice Statistics*, it finds that, *"93% of juvenile sexual assault victims know their attacker. 34.2% of attackers were family members. 58.7% were acquaintances. Only 7% of the perpetrators were strangers to the victim."* We realize that the perpetuators are in close proximity to their young victims and as in my case, my perpetuator was right in my own house. As reported by the *Child Mistreatment Survey,* " *In 1995, local child protection service agencies identified 126,000 children who were victims of either substantiated or indicated sexual abuse. Of these, 75%*

were girls. Nearly 30% of child victims were between the age of 4 and 7." These numbers only reflect those incidents that are reported to authorities. Still, many go unreported. Yet, according to the *U.S. Department of Justice's National Crime Victimization Survey (NCVS)*, finds that, *"there is an average of 237,868 victims (age 12 or older) of rape and sexual assault each year."* Remember that only 237,868 victims reported the crime whereas numerous victims keep silent. In the same survey, it also reports that, *"Sexual assault is one of the most under reported crimes, with 60% still being left unreported"* (NCVS). I can only surmise that these numbers would double if all cases of sexual assault are reported to the proper authorities. Many victims are groomed to be molested or raped by many known by them. As was my case in point exactly.

My father lured me into our secret with treats like candy, cookies, and leftover lunchmeat and crackers. He always found ways to get me alone, and away from the house, and out of my mother's sight by finding places to take me in his car. Starved for affection, I began to crave more of my father's attention and affection that he secretly and willingly gave me. My soul was like a dry desert and his attention was the water in my desert. It was our little secret and he often reminded me that if anyone knew we would have to stop. How could I stop the only love I was receiving?

I was so starved for love, affection, and human touch that I welcomed every inappropriate touch from my father. He loved to rub my arm, legs, back, and between my legs inside my panties. He took special care not to insert his finger in my vagina (that would wait until he would be ready to teach me everything about grown up love). But he would caress my vagina with his large and rough hands. His favorite thing was to put me on his shoulders for a ride. He would position my body on his shoulders so that he could rub my vagina with the back of his head. To my little mind and body, it felt good to feel his head there. I liked this because it wasn't his hands. I would feel all warm inside and loved. It was his favorite thing to do with me because he could carry me like that for miles and his secret play would be undetected.

Sometimes a victim's body will become aroused during molestation, even so, it's still sexual abuse. Arousal and enjoyment during abuse does not mean the abuse did not happen. It merely means that the victim is human. The victim is embarrassed by the fact that they enjoyed what their victimizer does to them. When a very young child is molested, he or she is deceived into thinking that the molestation is a good secret and nothing is wrong with what is being done to you or even what you are feeling. There was no reference point for me being a young child.

My father often planned activities we could do alone so that we could engage in "our secret". These were times when he would "love" me in his special way: rubbing, grabbing, kissing or touching me under my clothes. I often had to take off my panties because they got in the way of his large hands. I didn't mind because it meant that he loved me more than the other children.

I remember my father teaching me to drive when I was twelve. He would have me get positioned so that while I drove, he could rub me between my legs. People in the neighborhood thought my father was wonderful for holding the wheel with me as I drove down the dusty roads. They didn't know the feelings I couldn't explain or that I wanted them to go on so that I could have this love that I wanted so desperately. For it was in those times that I could forget that my sister was dead because of me and that my parents had lost their best child. I could pretend that my world was wonderful as my father paid attention to me.

Along with keeping my Dad's secret, I was molested by two other male relatives; my fraternal grandfather and first cousin. I also hid my fraternal grandfather's secret, as well as my first cousin until now. My fraternal grandfather tried to molest me with his walking cane when I was seven years old and then he threatened to beat with the cane if I told anyone. One summer day, my parents sent my oldest brother, Luther, and me to our grandparents' home. My grandmother, Pearl, was out back washing and hanging clothes on the line. My grandfather told my brother to go play in the front yard. After my brother went outside, he told me to take off my panties and sit on the floor Indian style in front of him. It was then he tried to insert his cane inside me, but because I was only seven and a virgin it didn't break my hymen. He had made me take off my panties and then sit like an Indian on the floor in front of him with my legs open. My grandfather attempted to push his woodened cane inside. I cried quietly praying that someone or anyone would come through the door and recue me from this horrible old man. After a few frustrating attempts, he screamed at me to get up and put my panties on while telling me I was good for nothing. He was rough, impatient, and brutal unlike my father who was gentle. I never told my parents and he died without me ever telling anyone, actually this is the first time I have mentioned it. I hated him from then on and I always gave my parents a hard time whenever they tried to send me back down to my grandparents' house.

On the other occasion, my nineteen year old first cousin took me in the garden one day while his parents came to visit my parents. He convinced me to give him a hug as he lay under a tree. While hugging me, he began to rub me between my legs through my panties. He then took out his penis and pushed me over on the ground where he laid on his side and put his penis on my inner thigh while trying to insert it in my body, but he ejaculated very quickly before he could push himself in me. I felt this sudden hot liquid on me that felt sticky and nasty. I looked down and it looked like the whites of an egg and it made me feel filthy.

My first cousin begged me not to tell anyone and that he

wouldn't do it again it I kept this secret. It was a very horrible secret for a nine year old. He became an alcoholic and struggled with addiction for the rest of his life until he died. I never told anyone until now. I kept this secret from my father because I was afraid and I felt nasty. I never felt clean after these events. Even my father's touch began to feel horrible, but it was attention so I endured it because I needed his touch which meant he loved me.

I had hated what my grandfather and cousin did to me. I never visited him again. He was a mean and bitter man and to my child's mind I thought what he did to me was some form of punishment for me being bad. I kept his horrible secret too. I was happy the day he died and left this world. His wife wondered why I didn't cry when he died, but I was too happy. My father was always quiet and sad around his father. But he seemed happy that his father was dead too.

In our small town, the townspeople would notice how my father doted on me. They would remark on how much he loved his little girl. They never guessed the real truth. In my mind, I felt that since he was my father, it couldn't be wrong. After all, he was the adult and he knew right from wrong. Or did he? How could a little fearful girl know the power of a secret or the destruction of a secret? How could I understand the devastation those touches would echo throughout my life and the lives of others? How could I know that my view of sex would be forever distorted and damaged?

How could I reject the love, acceptance, and appreciation I was getting in those secret moments when those big hands touched, stroked or held me? How could I not crave the hot breath on my face when he would hold me? I longed for those times. It was it those times that I found the comfort and love that I craved. It was my time, it was love that I felt; it was our secret. It was a secret we shared for over nine years. I enjoyed the part of the molestation that involved cuddling, hugging, and being carried on his shoulders by my father. I liked our special times together because he belonged only to me. But then they began to take on another nature and this was questionable even for my young age. However, Dad convinced me that all daddies shared secrets like this with their very special girls. I was his special girl. I had no idea that our secret meant that I was being "molested".

I did not understand that what my father, grandfather and cousin did to me was sexual perversion. I could not distinguish sex from love at that time or for many years to come. My father said that what we did was good, but I couldn't tell anyone. Anything that is done secretly, I learned, is probably perversion. What is perversion? *Perversion is defined as "a diverting from the true intent or purpose; a change to something worse; a turning or applying to a wrong end or use" (Webster).* In the Bible, the word *"perversion" is used to define a deviation from righteousness in sexual behavior"* (Leviticus 18:23, Romans 1:27, Ephesians, Colossians 3:5). Sexual perversion then is the opposite of what God created to be good in the union of marriage between and male and female that has been perverted into that which does not fulfil the intended purposes of God. ***"Then God said, "Let Us make man in Our image, according to Our likeness; let them have dominion over the fish of the sea, over the birds of the air, and over the cattle, over all the earth and over every creeping thing that creeps on the earth." 27 So God created man in His own image; in the image of God He created him; male and female He created them. 28 Then God blessed them, and God said to them, "Be fruitful and multiply; fill the earth and subdue it; have dominion over the fish of the sea, over the birds of the air, and over every living thing that moves on the earth" (Genesis 1:26-28).*** A man and woman are the only people who can procreate after their kind. Any other sexual liaisons are perverted.

Therefore, being molested by my father, grandfather and cousin was sexual perversion; it was also incest. Incest is defined as *"sexual intercourse between two persons commonly regarded as too closely related to marry"* (Webster). In the bible in 2 Samuel 13:1-15, King David's son, Amnon raped his own sister Tamar in the Bible; this is called incest (2 Samuel 13:1-15). There is nothing new under the sun, even rape occurred in the Bible. For me, I was plague with the thought that this only happened to me and that I was an outcast.

In the nine years of being molested by three men who should have known better, God kept His hands on me. The Bible reveals a powerful truth about secrets that I would learn after giving my life to

God in Deuteronomy 29:29, it says, **"The secret things belong unto the LORD our God: but those things which are revealed belong unto us and to our children for ever, that we may do all the words of this law." (Deuteronomy 29:29) (NKJV).** I kept destructive secrets for nine years as I was being molested until I turned fourteen. *"A child who is the victim of prolonged sexual abuse usually develops low self-esteem, a feeling of worthlessness and an abnormal or distorted view of sex. The child may become withdrawn and mistrustful of adults, and can become suicidal" (NCVS).* There was immense damage done to me due to my molestation and rapes. Many times victims of sexual abuse often live with emotions that keep them in bondage to the wounds of molestation and their ability to trust is destroyed. Most of my life it has been difficult to trust people and sometimes I could not fully trust God. Mistrusting God delayed my deliverance and healing from emotional and sexual abuse.

Corine H. Stone

CHAPTER 5
RAPED TWICE - TWO MEN - SAME DAY

It was the fall of 1967, I had turned fourteen (which was the age my father was waiting to arrive) and I was old enough to do all the special things my father wanted to do with me. I was always confused by this acknowledgement, but all I knew is I craved and enjoyed the attention being given to me by my father. Over and over, I wondered if this is what fathers and their little girls did; if grandfathers did to their granddaughters, and if this is what all cousins do to their little cousins. Yes, first it was a father, then a grandfather, a cousin, then finally a classmate and finally a family friend.

The most exciting thing about being fourteen was that I finally got my period. My friend from school, Johnnie Mae had found me sobbing in the bathroom at school because of the blood in my panties. She gently explained that I wasn't dying or that I had not done anything wrong. Johnnie Mae got all the things I needed from the office and explained what I needed to know. Most of all, she reiterated over and over that now I was a woman and that I could get pregnant if I had sex. "What is sex?" She told me not to worry and she would tell me tomorrow. Well tomorrow came and I wished it hadn't. After her description of sex, I just knew I never wanted to do this sex thing. It sounded so nasty.

By this time, my mother had a full time job at Helena Hospital working as a Certified Nursing Assistant; her hours were seven in the evening until seven in the morning. She instructed me to take care of the house and my siblings when I came home from school which meant cleaning, cooking, washing, etc. I thought I was doing a good job helping my mother while she worked to make ends meet. My father would leave in the mornings around five-thirty and retuned at six in the evening.

One cold wintery night, I was awakened by my father as he was attempting to get in my bed. He was dressed only in his white underwear. I noticed the budge in his underwear, the same kind my first cousin had when he tried to invade my privates. Suddenly, my father jumped in my bed and got under the covers with me. This was the first time he had come to my bedroom at home. Our activities had always been confined to outside the house. Well, he started grabbing me and quietly telling me to not scream. I struggled with him as he rubbed his hands over my small breasts while reaching between my legs. I screamed at him saying, "No, Daddy, please don't do this!" I said it over and over. I thought to myself about my school friend who explained sex. I knew I did not want to do this sex thing with my father.

I noticed the smell of beer on his breath and I hated my father in that moment and I just wanted him to leave my bed and room. My father became angrier as I fought and wrestled with him. He kept telling me I was old enough, big enough and ready to do the big girl stuff. All I could remember was what my friend Johnnie Mae said about getting pregnant. I found a new strength to fight him. After a few minutes, my father gave up and got out the bed. He stood over me and threatened. He said, "If you tell your mother or anyone, I will do the same thing to your sisters." They were asleep in the room next door, and I didn't want him to do that to them, to hurt them or do the things to them he had already done to me. He bought my silence.

I was silent for three years. My father left me alone for good. I wasn't his special little girl anymore. Weeks later, it was obvious to me that he hated me now because of his cold demeanor toward me. When I spoke to him, he only grunted at me. Sadly, I craved his familiar touch, a hug, something that said, "I still love you!" Abused victims often enjoy the attention and touch of their abusers even though on one hand they despise their touch. The body often betrays their repulsion which is conflicting in the minds of victims of sexual abuse. For a child who is being victimized by their father, it is even more troublesome. You are supposed to love your father but in the mind of a child how do you suppose to feel when your father is abusing you in a sexual manner? I did not know during those years that I was being sexually abused. I saw it as love. Neither did I understand that my view of love would forever be tarnished and distorted. Even any positive view of sex was tragically damaged.

My life seemed too horrible to live as I lived under the same roof with my father. Surprisingly, I was missing those private times we used to have. Since he was not spending time with me, I wondered what he was doing after nine years of secrets with me. Even still I continually watched over my sisters for any signs that he was trying to mess with them. When one of my younger sisters lost her voice for a whole year and would always sleep in a closet; and my other sister escaped our home at sixteen by running away to get married, I wondered if these events occurred because my father may have had special secrets with them as well. They both have said nothing happened to them. I thank God, but I still wonder if they have buried what happened to them like I had. All three of my sisters have denied that our father touched them in any sexual manner. I pray that is the truth.

In 1968, I was a fifteen year old sophomore in high school. I was smart, intelligent, and pretty much a loner. I didn't have a lot of friends in school. I didn't feel comfortable around people because I thought they would somehow find out my secret. My classmates mostly laughed at my skinny frame, skinny legs, and short thin hair. I only weighed ninety-eight pounds and my body had not developed like the other girls. My peers reminded me daily that with skinny legs, short, thin hair and no breasts that no one would ever want me for a girlfriend. Most of the girls had boys that were crazy about them, except me. The boys knew my parents were strict, so they did not bother to show an interest in me. I secretly had a crush on one of the seniors at school who had told me a few times that I was cute, smart, and intelligent. He was cute, tall, brown-skinned, and seventeen years old. This guy was the smartest guy in the senior class. He did not pay any particular attention to me anymore because he liked another girl at school. Until one day we were both in the hallway during class.

On this particular day, I had asked my teacher if I could be excused so I could go to the bathroom. It was 10:30 a.m. As I left the class, I had almost bumped into the popular senior that I liked. He spoke to me and I was speechless for a few seconds. He asked me if I could talk a minute. Delighted by his attention, I said, "Yes". Smiling, happy for once that he paid me some real attention. Thrilled that he was talking to me, I slowly strolled down the hallway as he talked to me. I felt beautiful, important, and special because of his attention. As we neared the auditorium, he said that he wanted to show me something, we entered the auditorium.

Once we entered the auditorium there was another door and he grabbed the doorknob and said, "Come on, girl". It was slightly dark in there, but I felt safe so I went in and he closed the door behind him. He grabbed me by the waist and pulled me to him and attempted to kiss my lips. I didn't like the way he grabbed me or the way he was trying to kiss me. I pushed him away, but the senior grabbed me again and began to pull my dress up over my head with one hand while trying to kiss me to stop my screams as he tore my panties off me. He wrestled me to the floor of the closet, swiftly climbed on top of me; and he forced my legs apart with his strong legs. The senior overpowered me and forcibly tore into me, ripping my soul with his brutal pounding in my body for what seemed like an hour. Suddenly, within what seemed like a lifetime, his body became stiff, he moaned, and then he fell limp on me for a brief time. I felt a warm wetness leaking from between my legs. It reminded me of what happened with my first cousin did to me when I was younger. Hot tears fell from my eyes. I felt worthless, filthy, useless, and violated. He had violated me in the worst way possible. Standing up, fixing his clothes; he looked at me with such loathing, and threatened me not to tell anyone or he will say I gave it up to every boy in school. Then he was gone. I lay there on the floor of that closet for hours it seemed. I was embarrassed and ashamed. I felt like I had been torn apart. I knew I had to be bleeding too. I was a mess. I gathered my torn panties and limped to the bathroom where I told everyone I was sick. I was messy, soiled and the tissue I used to wipe myself was bloody.

It felt like a knife had sliced my heart as well as my body. He hurt me so badly and humiliated me so much. I spent the rest of the day in a stall in the girl's bathroom feeling filthy, nasty, bruised, and degraded.

After school was over, I saw the senior with his friends. They were all laughing and I just knew they all knew what had happened to me. I kept thinking, "How could I ever come back to school again?" I was devastated, I felt worthless, humiliated, and unlovable. He had this look on his face like I was standing there naked. I cried quietly on the bus ride home. My friend, Juanita Edwards, questioned me and wanted to know what wrong with me. I couldn't tell her; I couldn't tell anyone! I believed that she and the others would think I was disgusting if I told her what happened.

As I rode the bus home in silence not believing the wretchedness of what happened to me or the horrible pains shooting through my lower part of my body. It felt like I was torn and ripped up on the inside of my womanhood.

Shame and misery flooded my soul. I blamed myself for craving the senior's attention. I knew I was to blame. I knew I had to be dying. It was a day I will never ever forget. That day, the rest of my innocence was taken away from me. I cried silently remembering that this must be what my father wanted to do to me. "Oh Lord, God, help me," I cried and cried because the pain in my body and soul was unbearable. I wanted to talk to someone, tell someone about this horrible nightmare that happened in the closet at school. I knew I couldn't stand for anything else to touch me down there. Or so I thought! I decided to talk to my cousin, Bessie, who lived a short distance from me down the road. I knew I could trust her.

Later that night I walked down the dirt road to my favorite cousin's house to talk to her because I knew I could tell her everything that had happened to me. My cousin was a year older; she was born January 29, 1952 and we were very close. Bessie was beautiful, smart and popular. She has a Coke Cola figure and all the boys were enamored by her beauty. What was so amazing about her to me – she had this walk, oh Lord, she walked like a model. It could get anyone's attention. But she always took the time to talk to me and I will always love her for taking time with her little cousin. Even though she passed away in September, 2003 from an aneurysm at fifty one years old; I will never forget her and how much we loved each other.

Bessie was like my big sister. I knew I could share anything with her and trust her. Once I got to her house, it all poured out of me. I cried and cried and she held me and told me it wasn't my fault. Bessie was so angry she wanted to tear the senior's head off. Angrily, Bessie ranted and raved how she was going to kill my rapist and cut his private part off and throw it out the school window as soon as she saw him. She held me, rocked me as I cried from the depth of my soul. Bessie never knew how I had fought my daddy for nine years, fought my grandfather, and my cousin to keep my virginity only to have it robbed and taken from me in such a degrading manner and at school in a closet by this horrible boy at school!

Bessie could never know the depth of my pain; never know how I had waged war against the men in my family who were supposed to love me the right way. So, I buried my rejection, shame and fear in the comfort of her warm arms and love. For over an hour she rocked me and stoked my hair until the sobs subsided. She told me over and over that she loved me and would be with me the next day as I went to our small country school that both my rapist and two of us attended. It was now a little after ten o'clock and time for me to go home. As my cousin walked me part of the way home, she encouraged me to tell my parents, but how could I tell them? I didn't have the courage or the strength to tell them. Plus, I didn't know what would happen when I told them. Would they blame me? Would they hate me? Would they whip me for agreeing to go in the closet with the boy? Would they blame me because I secretly liked the senior? I wasn't sure what to think or do. So, I took off down the road for home.

Waving to her, I rushed down the darkened rock road. Deep in thought, wondering how I could tell my parents what had happened to me; I passed by the one-room elementary schoolhouse I had attended for first through fifth grades. All of a sudden, out of the dark someone grabbed me from behind, putting his big, smelly hands over my mouth and dragging me up the school house stairs onto the porch of the school. In horror, I realized that it was my father's friend who would come by the house sometimes to drink beer with him. He threw me on the porch and slapped me knocking me to the floor of the porch. Like a lion, he was suddenly on top of me and he tore my panties and forced himself in me. The pain was so unbearable, I prayed for God to just kill me. I fought him; I tried to push him off me. He reeked of stale beer. He beard scratched my face. I felt sick to my stomach. It was useless. He raped me violently.

Raging pain began to rain in my body like a huge train was tearing quickly through my already ravaged body. I screamed, but no sounds came out. It was stuck in my throat. I prayed for death. It had been over as quickly as it started. When he slides his drunken body off me, I saw his face. Oh God, it was my father's friend, my classmate's father, my mother's friend's husband; he was the town's drunk and my second rapist in a twelve-hour period. He left me like I was a dirty tissue. He told me he would kill me and my family if I told anyone. I begged him to kill me now. He laughed and he pulled up his pants and stumbled off in the darkness. I was left in a heap on the porch. After finding tears from somewhere, I cried and cried. I was so sick to my stomach and I began to throw up over and over again. Finding the strength from somewhere, I dragged myself home. After making it home and saying goodnight to my parents, I ran water in the bathtub. Adding bleach to my bath water, I thought I would never feel clean again. My private was on fire as I lowered myself in the tub, but it didn't compare to the pain in my heart and soul. After spending an hour in the tub, I threw myself in the bed wishing that I had never been born.

I don't have the words to describe the devastation I suffered in that twelve-hour period. I am not sure how I lived through being raped twice in the same day. All I knew was that as I drifted off to sleep that night I wished I could go to the cemetery located a quarter of a mile down the road and dig a hole, jump in it, and cover myself up. "Death," I pleaded, "Please take me, now!" Of course, death had taken the night off and didn't hear my cries for his company.

I returned to school the next day a shattered and broken girl. I was withdrawn, quiet, and sad. I was only a shadow of the person I had been the day before. My teachers noticed and asked me what was wrong. I smiled and said I was alright. But every time I saw my first rapist, I cringed, and I would disappear in my mind by imagining that I was in a faraway place somewhere beautiful where I was happy and loved. That's how I dealt with seeing him, I disappeared. But Bessie wanted to fight him. She would roll her eyes at him as she passed him in the halls. I pleaded with her not to do anything because then people would find out what happened. I could not bear that to happen.

I cannot describe the depth of the effects of my being raped twice on the same day and by two different men who were familiar to me. According to a survey by the *World Health Organization*, the statistics on the effects of rape on victims find that they are: 3 times more likely to suffer from depression, 6 times more likely to suffer from post-traumatic stress disorder, 13 times more likely to abuse alcohol, 26 times more likely to abuse drugs, and 4 times more likely to contemplate suicide." To say that I was in a state of confusion and depression is understandable. How could I face anything more? There were some surprising symptoms I was now noticing about myself.

Now I had another secret to keep. Keep it, I did. My walk changed. It hurt now to walk. After two months, my body changed, now

I was growing breasts. No amount of baths made me feel clean enough. I just felt nasty all the time. I kept both rapes from my parents and tried to live through the tears, rips, bruises that had been left by my attackers. I had a greater problem facing me. I noticed that I was sick a lot in the mornings. My mother noticed too.

Two and a half months later she decided to take me to the doctor to see what was wrong with me.

CHAPTER 6
BLANKETED IN THE SPIRIT OF SHAME

The doctor informed my mother that I was ten weeks pregnant, and that I had been severely raped and that it seemed like that's when I got pregnant. "Pregnant?" The doctor told my mother. Pregnant, pregnant, I thought, that's something you get after you get married. "Severe vaginal tearing, deep bruising, untreated, prescribe medication, take three times a day, vitamins, iron pills too, come back in two weeks," the doctor continued telling my mother. My mother's face turned white and it looked like stone. I was petrified. I knew she was going to kill me.

Finally, after being questioned by my mother, I told my mother what the senior did to me. The doctor confirmed what I had told my mother. I saw her shoulders slouch; then she lifted her head and said, "It's going be alright, let's go." She further told me not to worry and that she would deal with the situation with the senior's mother. Shame flooded my soul as I sat there watching my mother wrestle with the weight of this entire situation. My shame bent me over and I walked out the doctor's office with my head hung low feeling such condemnation, not from my mother but from myself.

After getting in the car, I didn't tell her about the second rape for two major reasons. First, the second rapist was a friend of my parents and I felt my mother would have killed him. Second, I did not believe that he was the reason I was pregnant. Somehow deep within me, I felt that the baby belonged to the first rapist.

Since the doctor's office was only a mile away from where the senior lived with his family, my mother drove me directly to his mother's house. Making a right turn across the railroad tracks and driving the mile down the rock road, my mother pulled up in front of the first rapist's house. The speckled, grey haired lady who answered the door said she was the senior's mother. The woman seemed indifferent and uncaring as my mother began speaking with her. My mother looked like she wasn't taking anything from anyone. She was ready to tear somebody's head off right then. She had a slight temper and if this woman knew what I knew, she had better come correct with Mrs. Williams.

My mother said to the senior's mother, Mrs. Richardson, "Your boy done got my daughter in trouble, what you going to do about it?" His mother quickly said, "Nothing, cause my boy going to college and he ain't done nothin' to nobody, especially her!" His mother's eyes wandered over me and my body with such contempt. My mother told me to go to the car. I was glad to leave that house, the air was stiffing. His mother eyes followed me out to the front door and continued denying to my mother that her son was to blame for my pregnancy. As I balled up in a knot in the front seat of the car, intense feelings of shame like waves on an ocean washed over me. In my mind, I felt that even his mother thought I was worthless.

My mother appeared in the door of Mrs. Richardson's house. I was relieved that she was leaving as I watched them from my mother's car. Both women were loud. They were screaming at each other as they exited the house and were now standing in the front yard. When my first rapist heard his mother's voice rising, he suddenly appeared in the doorway and caught the last of his mother's words. "Ma, I swear, I ain't done nothin' to her, I swear, I promise," he screamed. "She is lying on me!"

Each pronouncement of his denial entered my ears in slow motion in all capital letters. Shame crashed through my innermost being. I felt like I was smothering, I couldn't breathe. I thought back to the day before he raped me, I remember him telling me as we walked in the hallway at school that, "You're cute", but all the time he never cared for me. Remembering how he never spoke to me after that day in the closet, never acknowledged me at school, never came near me, never acted like I was alive; and I clutched my heart and my throat. I closed my eyes hoping to block out what I was seeing and hearing.

Inside my mother's car I prayed to God, "Open the ground, let the earth swallow me, erase me from my mother's memory; let her forget my birth, my name, my life, kill me, kill me, God. Why didn't God let me die in the fire? I wanted death. Death, where are you when I need you?" I did not feel that I was worth the air I breathed. I wanted to just die, disappear, or just have God erase me off the face of the earth like I had never been born. I quietly prayed, "Take me, God, I am ready". God was quiet that day or so I thought.

My mother got into the car said softly, "Tell people I am the baby's daddy." She drove off as if to say, "Nough said!" And that's how it was; I was the mama and my mother was my baby's daddy. Later, she would tell my father about my pregnancy, and I ceased to exist in his eyes. His disdain for me was heartbreaking. It felt as if he had been cheated out of being the first to have that moment with me. After he learned that I was pregnant, my father ignored me as if his prized possession had been tarnished in his eyes. I became invisible to him.

Denying the rape, my rapist's mother and family stood firmly behind my initial rapist. Rejecting me and the fluttering sensation of life in my stomach; he left me to carry the weight of my shame now compounded with rejection and fear. My mother decided to let life judge him and chose not to bring charges against him because she didn't want our community to know what had happened to me. I welcomed the relief of her wise decision.

Devastated during the entire pregnancy, I crouched in the comfort of my home clutching my growing belly and drawing strength from the life I carried in my womb. As my baby grew larger so did my reason to live. For now I had someone who would belong to me and who would love me back. I had to live so that this being who was tied to my soul could live and love me; something I had wanted all of my life.

But my mother had another plan for the baby growing inside me. Her plan provided me with an escape from the stares and questions from the residents of my hometown. I was headed for the shelter waiting for me in Illinois. My mother sent me to live with one of her younger sisters, Auntie Annie Mae and her husband, Uncle Joe. They lived in Chicago and they had a cute, little, six year old daughter, Deborah who had thick, long ponytails.

My aunt, her husband, along with her young daughter and her brother, Uncle Eddie, embraced me upon my arrival. She and my uncles provided for my care and education throughout the rest of my pregnancy. They loved and never judged me. Having only the one child, I knew they wanted another child. We talked often about my life after my delivery. I came to believe that it was best for my unborn child if I gave him to my aunt and her husband to adopt. I knew they would love him and give him a better life than me. This decision was heart wrenching for me. I felt that sometimes when you love someone you will let them go if it's best for them. I felt they could give him a happier home and life than me. They were excited and began to prepare for the baby in my womb that would become theirs.

I became a mother after two days of labor, fifty-four stitches and fourteen days before my sixteenth birthday on Tuesday, January 28, 1969 at 6:00 p.m. My wonderful, bouncing son was born in Mt. Sinai

Hospital on the Westside of Chicago. He was a beautiful, healthy six pounds and twelve ounce bundle of joy. When the nurse laid him in my arms, I felt warmth in my heart that I had never felt before. A brilliant love began to gush out of my heart for the little bundle of joy in my arms. I felt a surge of protection rush through me and all I wanted to do was shield him from all the bad things in life that had tried to destroy me. I instantly loved my son as I drank all of him into my heart. He was so easy to love. I have never known a love like that before in my life and it felt so refreshing and so good to me.

The birth of my precious son changed my journey. I now had a reason to live. After praying for years to die without success; my son caused me to want to live again. When he grabbed my finger as I held him right after delivery, I knew that God loved me and had given me this awesome gift so I would want to live. I knew I could never give him up for adoption to my aunt and uncle. Disappointed, my aunt and uncle accepted my decision and they never skipped a beat in their undying love and devotion to me or my son. I walked out the hospital three days later as a fifteen year old mother holding a six pound, powerful reason to live and not die!

My son, Victor LaShawn, bought so much joy into my life. Victor loved me unconditionally. His love enfolded me and gave me a safe place to breathe and finally to live. My son is the blessing of my youth. I love him and he loves me. Joined and connected since his conception, we have grown up together as a mother and son loving and protecting our love and each other. Looking in his eyes and the smile on his lips brought comfort to my love-starved soul. I prayed to God thanking Him for understanding and giving me a strong, happy son who was my love, my heart, and my purpose in life. He is my "gift" from God that helped to erase my pain. God has blessed me despite all that I had been through. I give God all the glory. Some may wonder if he is a reminder of what happened to me, the answer is "No!" He is my gift from God and a reminder of how much God loves me and him. When I love at my son, all I see if love and happiness!

My son and I returned to Arkansas to my parents' home after the doctor cleared me to travel. My mother and siblings adored Victor and he became the apple of their eyes. He went from my mother's arms to each of my siblings' arms. Everyone loved this smiling baby who could melt the coldest heart. But my father kept his distance from my son and me. That was fine with me now because I had someone who loved me.

Having my baby was great for me, but, on the other hand, it was very conflicting and challenging for me because by now I was a sixteen year old mother who still had two years of high school to finish. Girls normally did not become mothers and then return to school in my hometown; but I was allowed to return to my high school. Classmates and friends were encouraged by their parents and peers to avoid me so they would not get a reputation.

More rejection and shame occurred after returning to tenth grade. Boys and men assumed a teenage mother was easy prey and willing to engage in sex without much hassle. Yet, on the inside I feel very much like a teenager and I just wanted to be a regular sixteen year old. What was conflicting was the fact that I was raped. I did not just have sex; it was forced upon me. I had planned to lose my virginity on my wedding night. I was misunderstood and became a teen outcast in my hometown. Feeling like "a scarlet teen" I tried to fade into the fabric of my small country town. I wanted to grow up and flee the harsh community.

After returning to school, I made some questionable choices by looking for love in all the wrong places. I knew my son loved me, but I made some decisions that were absolutely bad for me. I was looking for love and the other people were looking for just sex. It took a while for me to learn the difference. There are some decisions and choices that I made during this time that are embarrassing and painful. It is also shameful. Not only was I struggling with rejection, now add shame and fear to the situation. Due to my feelings of worthlessness, I allowed myself to fall into some ridiculous situations. I asked God to forgive me and He did. I thank God for the blood of Jesus because I knew I didn't belong on a path of promiscuity. I know the enemy wanted me to be a slut, but God wanted me to preach His word!!

After a year of foolishness, I realized finally that I wanted more out of life for my son and me. I had issues and that my issues had issues. Yet, I didn't quite understand that I was suffering from rejection, shame and fear, and I had found myself making compromises and lowering my standards just for a few moments of thrills only because I needed attention, acceptance, and approval. Like Apostle Paul said, **"For what I will to do, that I do not practice; but what I hate, that I do" (Romans 7:15b).** Admittedly, I struggled with the spirit of rejection to the point that I did things that I hated and detested just for brief moments of attention and supposed affection. The thing I didn't want to do that's what I found myself doing. But God!! I thank God for never leaving me. Even in the midst of my mess, God had His hand on me and He constantly reminded me of the call He had on my life. I was born for purpose, God's purpose. Rejection, molestation, rape, and shame were Satan's weapons of choice to destroy me. These weapons did not take me completely out. However, I learned that Satan still had other tricks up his proverbial sleeve.

Corine H. Stone

CHAPTER 7
ENGULFED AND BOUND BY FEAR

Nearly two years after the birth of my son, I was still struggling with some of my issues. My greatest struggle was fear; I was afraid to tell my mother about my father and what he had done to me from age five to fourteen. I had such a strong impulse to tell my mother because since I had returned home with my son, I was scared to be in the house at night with my father when my mother was working. I just did not know how I could tell her or know where to get the strength to tell her something like that about her husband and my father.

Have you ever felt like giving up or felt like asking God to just take you home? These questions have raged in my heart all my life. God, why me? Why Shirley, why not me? Why wasn't I the one who died? Why am I here, Lord? Why, Lord, why? I felt that I didn't have the right to be alive. I should be dead. Feeling like I should exchange places with my beautiful sister and friend. Lord, God, help me. I asked God over and over again, "Why, Lord, why?" Or have you asked the infamous question, "Why me"? "Well, why not you"? That's what God spoke in my spirit one night as I prayed to die, to leave this place that has caused me great pain at seventeen; an age when life seemed to hold so much promise – I wanted to cover myself in a grave not far from my home.

After returning home with my son, my father would continue to get drunk and become mean while my mother was at work. He wandered from bedroom to bedroom. I feared he would start the molesting again. Feeling uncomfortable with my mother being out of the house and my father's occasional walks through my bedroom, I began running away at night when my father would drink thinking that he would come in my room to rape me. I would put my sleeping baby in my younger brother's bed and I would slip out the house. I would return home minutes before my Mom's car headlights turned on the road by our house. Most of the time, I was right outside on the back porch or on the side of the house. Other times I found comfort in my mother's good friend, Liz Brown Walker's house down the road.

This went on for two years until Liz, my mother's friend and co-worker, asked me why I couldn't stay at home at night. I was seventeen by now. Finally, I told her my secret, which tumbled out like a broken dam searching for a place of understanding and love. Expecting unbelief, rejection, and more condemnation; she cried as I cried; she understood and she believed me. I felt an amazing comfort after having carried my horrible secret most of my life. My secret had come home to rest on the heart of another human being and she did not hate me, as I had feared.

Feeling safe, I felt finally a freedom in my tortured soul that I had not ever felt. I wanted to live with her the rest of my life. Liz said that she needed to go to my grandmother so that she could help us with the next steps. I knew my grandmother loved me; I knew that she would do everything to protect me. I knew she loved me and would not blame me. Grandmothers have a way of knowing things; a wisdom that comes from God.

Immediately, Liz drove me to my grandmother's house where I fell in her lap crying that blistering kind of cry where all you want is relief. Grandma knew exactly what to do. I breathed a sigh of relief. It didn't last long. I felt her draw several deep breaths. I felt her rub my head. I felt her tears drop into my hair as she whispered, "Lord, Lord!" Suddenly, she told me to go wash my face because we were going to my mother's house. It was just getting dark outside. Kids were running, playing, jumping rope as if life was fine, like they could not see that I just wanted to scream, die, runaway whichever came first. I got in my grandmother's truck, hugging Elizabeth and thanking her for everything, looking into her eyes searching for salvation, wanting to be saved from this truck ride. "God, please help me," my soul seemed to scream. I was terrified at what my grandmother would say to my parents; terrified of what my father would say and finally, and terrified at what my mother would say and do?

My grandmother walked in the house first with me following close behind her. I was praying that she would shield and protect me from my parents. She called my mother's name as she entered from the kitchen. Grandmother asked her where my father was and she said out back. My grandmother said, "I need to talk to both of you." My mother looked confused and uneasy. She asked me, "Where you been girl?" I looked at my grandmother who said, "Just get him and we need to go into the back room." My siblings were sitting on the floor watching television. Dad came in looking sheepish and boyish, grinning. "How are you doing, Ma?" Grandmother said, "Not good right now!"

My parents, grandmother, and I went into my bedroom located in the back of the house. My parents sat on the bed and I stood behind my grandmother. My grandmother did not waste any time. She said, "Your daughter got something to tell you." With a small voice, I told my mom what my daddy had done to me beginning at age five until I was fourteen. As I talked my voice got stronger with my Grandma holding my hand. I felt her tremble with anger.

My mother looked like life was standing still and her eyes were stone cold. Unbelief ran across her face as she looked at my dad and then me. My daddy standing near the dresser hung his head. My mother screamed a weird kind of scream I had never heard before; it did not seem like it would ever end. She screamed, "You lying heifer, I don't believe you. You are lying. Why you lying on your daddy like that. I ought to whip your butt…"

Suddenly my father shouted, "I did it, I did it. The child is telling the truth." My mother looked at him and she screamed, "You stop lying, stop it, stop it." He said, "She is telling the truth I did it. I am sorry." My mother fell across my bed sobbing like I had so many times in the same bed where he had attempted to forced himself on me. She sobbed so loudly; it felt like a storm was rushing through the shotgun house. I was petrified with fear as my mother cried so tumultuously.

My mother cried and cried. Somehow, I began to blame myself once again for my mother's pain. I had hurt her for not dying instead of Shirley. Now I had hurt her again with my secret. The pain of hurting and disappointing the woman who had given me life was torturing my whole being. Thinking to myself that somehow it was my all fault for what my daddy did and for how I made my mother hate me. I cried but my tears were too hot to fall outside my eyes; they spilled over inside my heart, which seemed to be broken in a million pieces.

Lifting her head from my bed, she looked at me and she screamed at her mother, "Get her out of my sight, I can't bear the sight of her; get her out of my house." I shook my head thinking that my ears and eyes had stopped working. I looked at my grandmother, her mouth was moving but I couldn't hear the sounds coming out of it.

Suddenly, Grandma said, "You fool, you crazy fool. The man said he did it, why are you getting rid of her and not him?" My mother said, "Get her out of here, now!" My grandmother looked as if her own daughter had slapped her. Turning to me she said, "Get your stuff, I am taking you home with me, hurry get what you need, you are going with me."

By this time my father was embracing my mom as she sobbed uncontrollably on my bed. He was rocking her and strangely to me she was holding onto him as if for dear life. A picture of total fear, rejection and dejection imprinted itself on my heart as I gathered my things and my baby and left my parent's house. My self-esteem plummeted and registered zero that day. Feelings of worthlessness and terror flooded my being as I rode to my grandmother's house. I wanted death to claim me this time for the last time. What was the purpose of living? How could I live after today?

After seeing my mother cling to my molester, my whole being throbbed with pain and rejection by the two people charged with loving me. What a choice to make, a daughter or a husband. Oh God, kill me please. Let my heart stop beating now. It did not seem that I could survive the pain of betrayal by my poor heart.

I was surprised when the bright sun suddenly appeared through the sheer curtains of my bedroom the next day finding once again that I was still here; still alive. Oh, no, God! How could anything be worse?

I was engulfed in fear and I prayed to God asking him for "deliverance" from this horrible pit. I prayed for my friend, Death, to take me from it all. Feelings of unworthiness plagued me to the core. By now I was begging death to become my best friend. Death would be a friend I could talk to and beg to take me away from the life I was living.

I disappeared this time, I forgot who I was. I forgot my name. I forgot it all. I had a nervous breakdown. I escaped the pain. I had escaped to a place in my mind where there was no pain. Even though I could hear my family talking, I could hear my grandmother pleading with me to talk, I could hear the doctors; I couldn't. I wouldn't because the place I disappeared had sunshine and no heartaches. I felt warm, safe, loved. I was happy in my garden of flowers and beautiful trees and blue vibrant waters. Things smelled wonderful. I was happy. My disappearance lasted a week. I missed my son. I needed him so I came back for my son, my reason for living. I knew I couldn't stay in that place, I had to reappear. I had to come to some frightening conclusions from my past.

I realized that keeping my father's secret had done a lot of damage to me emotionally. But now in my seventeen year old mind; I realized that it had all been wrong. But I had been powerless as an innocent child to stop it because I felt that I needed those feelings of being loved even if it was by my own father. In my mind, it appeared that my only way to escape fear was to die. However, Mrs. Annie, my grandmother had another plan for my life. She decided that her oldest granddaughter was going to live and not die! My son and I moved to her house. In her safe haven I began to believe in her prayers and was able to shed enough fear to the point that I wanted to live again - for my son. Yet, there was a longing in my soul for another kind of love.

It was then that I began to long for someone tangible that

belonged to me. I had my son and grandmother, and I had a few girlfriends that had to be careful about being seen with me. How do you verbalize a feeling that you have never had before in life? I dreamed of long talks, walks, music, dancing, picnic, car rides, and someone to experience it with who would be bold enough to claim me as their own. It was a longing deep within me that craved a close connection with another human being.

CHAPTER 8
SEARCHING FOR LOVE IN ALL THE WRONG PLACES

"He who finds a wife finds a good thing, and obtains favor from the Lord" (Proverbs 18:22)

The wise writer of the Book of Proverbs wrote that when a man finds a wife he, indeed, finds a good thing. It is the man - according to the Bible- who searches for the wife. Most assuredly, I learned much later in life that when the woman finds a man; she loses. With this mindset, I set out in my life after the devastating confession of my father and sequentially my mother's betrayal to find me a man who would love me. Therefore, fool heartily; I embarked on a quest that would turn my life upside down several times for many years. My quest began not far from my parents' home, on the verge of my eighteenth birthday. My quest became a cycle that repeated itself down through the years. In hindsight, I have now learned that a cycle will not change until healing takes place. Being stubborn and the rebel that I was, I made up my mind that I was going to live my life - my way. All I can say is, it cost me more than I meant to pay.

I am not sure why, but I returned home to my parents' after a few months of living with my grandmother. Upon my return, I discovered that a new family moved to my community. I was almost eighteen and in the twelfth grade. My son was almost two and I was dreaming of graduating and returning to Chicago so I could go to college to get my teaching degree. I wanted to become an English teacher.

The Glass family was large, but they had one son who would become my first love. Born June 3, 1951, Paul Issac Glass was six feet tall, dark, and handsome. Because he was twenty-one years old, my mother said Paul was too old for me. He had the most beautiful, perfect, white teeth. Paul had deep dimples in his chiseled cheeks. His skin looked like oil and was very handsome to me. He had a wonderful way of lighting up the house when he visited me after he came from work. He was the first man who took an interest in me with no hidden agenda. It was exciting and thrilling to me to have this man, not a boy, talk to me and ask me questions about me, my son, and life. He called me "Orine". He often told me that I was his angel who fell from heaven. He made me feel alive, special and beautiful. Each day after work, Paul showed up at my parents' house with Chips Ahoy Chocolate Cookies and two cartons of milk for me and Victor. That melted my heart.

By age eighteen I was in love for the very first time with this man I called a gentle giant. Of course, my parents objected to the relationship for various reasons, but mostly because he had left school to help support his family after his father became ill. My mother forbade me to talk to him, but I disobeyed her anyway because he was my only friend who wasn't ashamed of being seen with me. He was his own man and he wasn't afraid of my parents. Paul was the first man who loved me and who only wanted to make me happy; never asking me for anything in return. I felt secure in my feelings for him because they were reciprocated.

During the early summer, Paul proposed to me. He asked me to run away with him so we could get married. I waited until my parents were sleep and I took my son and we slipped out the house in the middle of the night. Paul was waiting for me. It was a Friday night. He took me to his sister's house and I spent the night there. The next morning Paul arrived and picked me and Victor up. We were on our way out the door so we could go to the courthouse to get married. But as we stepped outside, my mother pulled up to the front of the house. She blocked the driveway. Paul put his arms around me and told me not to be scared and that it was going to be ok.

Getting out the car, my mother screamed at me, saying I was acting like a tramp because I had been shacked up with a no good man all night. I ran down the steps and told her it was not true. I told my mother that Paul didn't stay with me last night. Finally, I said, "We are on our way to get married right now." My mother said, "Over my dead body." She was so angry, so was I. My mother told me to get myself in the car right now because I wasn't getting married. She grabbed me, I was holding my son's hand, and she shoved us in the car. I had enough and I screamed at her. I told her, "I hate you and I wish you were dead!"

My mother clutched her heart and slumped in the front seat of her car. Tears flowed down her eyes.

I was devastated to see her tears. I hugged Paul and told him that I was sorry and that I was going with my mother. He squeezed me tightly and kissed my head and hair. He said he loved me and that we would get married soon. I took my son and we got in the back seat of her car and she drove off. I looked back through the back window and Paul was crying. As my mother drove down the street all three of us in the car was crying. My mother was crying because of the harsh words I had said to her. I was crying because she was destroying my opportunity to be with the man I loved. Victor was crying because the two women he loved most in the world were crying. I felt so bad for Paul. He didn't deserve this treatment from my mother. He was the kindest man in the whole world to me. She just didn't know him. He was good, kind, gentle and respectful to me and my son.

Paul never thought he was smart enough or had enough to offer me; but what he did not know was just his being brave enough to love me made him good enough for me. He didn't back down when my father would look at us or make snide comments. After our failed attempt to get married, it was difficult to live in the house and hide the truth about my feelings for Paul, but I did. My parents forbade me from having anything to do with Paul. He was not welcome in our house. My mother told me she was sending me back to Chicago on the weekend - which was just five days away! My world was crumbling beneath my feet. Leave here, leave Paul! Never see Paul again!! How could I?

So, I asked my mother if I could take my son and go stay at my grandmothers for a few days so I could sort things out. She agreed. Secretly, I think she was happy because I would be several miles away from Paul.

A knock at my grandmother's door two days later, showed me that there were still pieces of my heart not completely broken.

Paul entered looking decisively troubled, his head hanging low. "What's wrong?" I asked. He had heard the news already, the news that I found so difficult to share with him.

Trying to muster up a smile, Paul said, "I know you are moving to Chicago; my little sister told me." He looked like he could hardly breathe as he released each word. Tears flowed down his chin and I sat in the swing whimpering like a wounded animal.

The night was calm and a gentle breeze blew on us. We held hands and our hearts said the words that our lips couldn't form. Our hearts understood even without the literal words. This was my rock that I had grown to lean on daily. He had listened to my dreams and dried many tears from my eyes. He had encouraged my dreams of going to college and becoming a teacher. He had my back. When I was with him, the rejection, shame, and fear disappeared from my spirit. I felt safe with Paul Isaac Glass.

As he poured out his heart and pain, all the words seemed to run together and sounded like a foreign language being poured out of a bucket. My heart felt like as if life was being crushed out. I felt lost, totally alone without a friend in the whole world. Who would I talk to, who would listen to me, how could I go through the days knowing that I would never feel the comfort of his smile? How could I leave him now? This is unbearable, but when I looked up into his eyes, it was if I was looking in a mirror. His pain was mirrored back to me.

Forgetting my selfishness and pain, I saw the tears roll down his cheeks that he was trying to hold back. Reaching up I touched his face gently and wiped his tears as they fell. Grasping my hand, my hand disappeared in the palm of his hand. He held my hand near his heart, which was beating wildly. He embraced me wrapping his arms around me and laying his head on my shoulder, we cried together. It was in that instant that his heart seemed to reveal to my heart his secret. He loved me and understood that I had to leave to achieve my goals of going to college, but the thought still hurt both of us.

I was storing in my mind all the details of his touch, his arms, his hands, his cologne, and his breath on my face as he embraced me. And always I remembered his husky voice that sounded like the music of a restless ocean.

"I love you, 'Orine, I love you," he said over and over. I love you too my heart sang and I melted in the curve of his strong arms. We made a million promises that night. We made promises to live by and promises that would keep us until we could hold each other again. Paul's touch was warm and comforting so very different from the other touches I had received from my father, grandfather and cousin. I drank in the moment that he held me. My heart swelled with love, with longing and with tears trying to figure out how I could go on without the comfort of his friendship.

As I watched him walk hesitantly away from me, I died over and over. I cried so hard that both my eyes swelled up and would not open the next morning. Each night I prayed for death to come take me to a better place. Any place was better than this pain. Daily what I remembered was Paul's back walking out of my world and disappearing in the dark.

I left home for good boarding the Greyhound Bus that would take me to Chicago and take me to the place far away from me pain. I left my son with my mother so I could get settled up north. We had never been apart, but he didn't understand that his mom was leaving for a short while. My heart bleed for my darling son and the man I loved. I moved to Chicago and moved in with another of my mother's sisters, Aunt MV. I was sad, lonely, but Chicago was bursting with excitement. I lived for the nightly phone calls to my son and Paul. We would cry on the phone for a long time and even cried over the operator asking him to add more money in the pay phone. Every day I cried continuously after I left my hometown, a familiar and painful place I had lived in for eighteen years and for the two guys I loved most dearly. I missed my son, Victor and my love, Paul, my best friend. My heart ached for them.

A week after arriving in Chicago, my mother called her sister warning her that Paul was on his way to Chicago to get me and not to allow him to see me. So when he arrived at my aunt's door, she called the police and they promptly showed up in a few minutes. Over her threats, he screamed for me to come with him and that he loved me, etc. But my aunt blocked the door refusing to let me go. I screamed and cried and repeatedly declaring that I hated my mother for what she just did. I begged my Aunt MV to let me go with Paul and that I loved him. She held her ground and kept him from entering her house.

The police arrived and threatened Paul saying that if he didn't leave that he was going to jail. Begrudgingly, Paul walked down the stairs. I ran to the window and watched him walk to his car. His shoulders were slumped and his head was hanging very low. My giant had been blindsided and seemingly cut off at his knees. For a brief moment, he turned and looked up at the window where I was standing above the street. Tears ran down his mustache and to his beard. I was blinded by hot tears. I will never forget the forlorn look in his eyes. It tore me up on the inside and I thought I would die. He left Chicago that day, but he never left my heart. And I know he never stopped loving me until the day he died. I never stopped loving him because he was my first love, my only love. The summer of 1971 was a painful and heartbreaking time for me.

In the years afterward our breakup, whenever I traveled home to Arkansas, he always sensed when I would come home. He would show up wherever I was with a big smile. We would spend countless hours talking about our lives and what would have happened if we had gotten married. We loved each other deeply. He was my first love.

My mother encouraged me to stay in Chicago and to let Paul go. She told me that I was beautiful and soon there would be someone who would come along and make me happy. As a matter of fact, one of her friend's sons had come by the house and he had asked about me. I knew him from Lakeview High School. My mother gave him my Chicago address and he said he would write me. Ezell wrote me. He was nineteen, dark, quiet and away in the Army. I wrote him back, but I didn't like him either. I was in love with Paul. I kept my letters friendly but he started calling me his girlfriend.

I got a job in my Auntie MV's hotdog stand on Central Park near Roosevelt Road on the Westside of Chicago. My younger fifteen year old cousin worked there with me. She was tall, cute, and thick. Since I was one hundred and five pounds, small and thin, she appeared to be the older one. So there was this older guy would come in every day after work and order his food. He was twenty-five years old. Freddie Hunt was a Vietnam Veteran with a caramel complexion and black glistering, wavy hair; he was five feet and ten inches. He was neatly dressed and very handsome to me. While he waited on his food, he was flirting with my little cousin. I interrupted him and told him to leave her along and that she was only fifteen. He said, "You are kidding, how old are you?" I told him I was eighteen. He shook his head and said he didn't believe me. My cousin Carolyn chimed in and said that, "She is eighteen and has a two year old son." Shocked, he looked at me. Freddie really looked at me. Suddenly, he said, "You cute! How about going to the movies with me?" I told him no.

After turning his date requests down several times, I decided that he might be perfect for me. So, on August 6, 1971, he took me to see an old Clint Eastwood movie, **"Hang 'Em High"**. We had a good time. He bought me popcorn, candy, hotdog, and a big coke. As I watched the movie I thought of the man I loved and I felt guilty. Somehow I knew my mother would never approve of Paul and me getting married, but I felt she would like Freddie. We began dating and we had fun. Freddie wasn't alarmed that I had a son and he said he couldn't wait to meet him.

I spent the rest of the summer loving, missing and talking to Paul on the phone nightly, dating Freddie, and writing Ezell. I told Freddie that I loved Paul and that my family didn't approve of him. Cocky and self-assured, Freddie said he didn't care and that Paul was hundreds of miles away. He was confident because I was there with him. I resolved to continue seeing Freddie, but that my heart would never belong to him. I even told him that I was writing a boy from back home that was in the Army. He said it didn't bother him. So that's how I spent the rest of summer.

I got a letter from Ezell late September and he was coming home on leave. He wanted to know if I could come home because he had a surprise for me. Immediately, I called my mother and read the letter. She was excited and told me to come on home. I hesitated for a minute and then I told her about my seeing Freddie. She said her sister told her about it and that he was a nice young man and she liked him for me. My mother said that was nice and to come on home and see how things went with Ezell before I made a choice. So I listened and took the Greyhound bus home to Arkansas. My stomach was filled with excitement during the eight hour bus ride, but not about Ezell.

During the bus ride to Memphis, I met a nineteen year old girl named Denise who was friendly and outgoing. We sat together and talked the whole way there. She shared with me her story about being pregnant and going back home to live after being tricked into a relationship with a man who turned out to be married with two kids. She was brokenhearted that her boyfriend deceived her. Of course, I told her my story about being in love with a guy my parents disapproved of, dating a mature guy back in Chicago and going home to see a guy whom my mother liked and approved.

After our bus arrived in Memphis, Denise and I both had to use the bathroom once we got our bags. As we chatted, we walked to the ladies room. I told Denise that I would watch her bags while she used the bathroom. When she came out, I handed her purse and suitcases. Then she said that she would watch all my things while I used the bathroom. I gladly gave her my things and I went into the next available stall. Coming out the stall, I didn't see Denise anywhere, but my suitcase was in the aisle of the bathroom and my purse was sitting on top of it. Grabbing my purse I looked in it. My wallet was still there. Opening my wallet, I saw that all my money was gone and all I had left was my ticket to West Helena from Memphis. I cried so hard that I fell out in the floor. I called my mother collect and told her. She told me that at least I still had my ticket and not to trust anyone else. After I called my mother, I called Freddie upset about losing all my money. He answered and listened to my story. He started fussing at me for trusting a stranger. I started crying. He apologized to me for fussing. What he says next shocked me. Freddie said, "What's your address there? I am going to send you two hundred dollars later today when I get off work." I said to him, "Are you kidding, you do know I came down here to see another guy and that I may never come back to Chicago?' He said, "I don't worry about it, I already know." I was truly flabbergasted. I thanked him and ran to catch the Continental Trailways' bus home.

My mother and son were waiting for me when the bus pulled into the bus station. My heart was overjoyed as I picked up my son and kissed him over and over. He hugged my neck for dear life. Oh God, I was so happy to hold my child. In my heart I declared that I would never leave him anywhere again. I was so thankful to my mother for caring for my son. I hugged her and told her I loved her. I really wanted to please my mother because I had hurt her in the past and I had taken away my sister, who was her angel.

Ezell called to check to see if I had arrived that night. He asked me to go the drive-in movies the next night. I agreed. Despite agreeing to go out with him, I called Paul and asked him to pick me up when my parents went to sleep. He picked me up at ten thirty that night. My heart was racing and my pulse was beating overtime. Oh God, when I saw Paul, he had the widest smile on his face. He was showing all his teeth.

Paul jumped out the car, ran towards me, picked me up, and swung me in the air. He put me down and stood me on the ground. My body melted into his and we stood holding on to each other for dear life. Both of us were now crying and saying how much we loved each other. After five minutes, we jumped in the car and took off to his house.

It was a night that will belong to us forever. To protect my reputation, Paul wouldn't let me go in his house. We stayed outside on the porch. Later he made us a pallet and we spent the rest of the night lying on the ground outside his house. We counted the stars and dreamed dreams of being married and having five children. He held my hand and made a million promises to me.

Paul and I had a bond that would never be broken no matter what. I loved him so much because he never insisted or even said anything to me about that word, "sex". That night, Paul never insisted that I kiss him because he knew I detested kissing because of my rape. He would kiss me on my face and gently on my lips (no open mouth kissing). He said he would wait until we were married when everything would be right. I couldn't help but love this wonderful man. He held me and demanded nothing. I wanted the night to never end. Before daylight he drove me home. He embraced me and kissed my face and lips, but his kisses were mingled with tears. My heart felt like it was going to burst. I asked him to run away with me, to take me from this place and marry me. He said that he wanted to ask my parents for me and that it would be better if they gave us their blessing.

Crushed I held him tighter and cried wretchedly. He pried my arms off and told me it was time to go in the house. It was the hardest thing I ever had to do. We embraced one last quick time and I dashed in the house. Everyone was still sleep. I went back to the window and Paul was leaning over the trunk of his car, sobbing. I grabbed the doorknob to go to him, but right then my son called out to me from his uncle's room. I released the door and checked on Victor. He just wanted to see me. I kissed him and went to my room. Checking the window again, Paul was gone. I was so devastated. I got in the bed with all my clothes on and pulled the cover over my head. Under the covers, I cried river of tears like there was no tomorrow. I felt like an elephant was standing on my heart. Paul, I moaned, "I love you…"

Getting up early the next morning, my mother was excited about my upcoming date that night. She made me a beautiful blue straight dress that accentuated my body. I looked and felt beautiful. Ezell arrived promptly at seven that evening and he really liked my outfit. He was the perfect gentleman; he opened the door for me and closed it after I got in the seat. My mother was watching and smiling. She was impressed. On the drive to the movies, he caught me up on what he had been doing in the army. Quietly looking out the window at the changing scenery, I was thinking of my love, slumped over the trunk of his car, crying. I glanced at this guy in his uniform who was probably thinking I was impressed; I wasn't. He would never know that I was only in this car because of my mother. I wanted to be with Paul.

Pulling into the drive-in movie, he paid for our movie and ordered our food. We parked and our waitress bought our food to the car. We ate and he kept talking, but I was not listening. My mind was on the night before when I was with Paul. I was bored and wanted to leave. After we ate the food, he got out the car to throw away the garbage. When Ezell returned, he suggested that we get in the back seat because we would be able to see the movie better. I got in the back seat but moved close to the door. As we watched the movie, Ezell moved closer and closer to me. I was feeling uncomfortable. I look out the window to the surrounding cars. Most of the people in the cars were kissing, hugging and doing whatever in the backseats of their cars. I heard Ezell tell me to relax and give him a kiss. My antennas go up and I am alarmed. He grabbed me suddenly and tried to kiss me. He ran his hand up my dress, I fought him, and we wrestled in the back seat. Somehow he managed to get on top of me and all the time pulling my dress up. I screamed and screamed until some guys showed up at the car window asking me if I was alright. Luckily, one of them was from my neighborhood. He threatened to whip Ezell if he didn't let me go. My friend opened the car door and I jumped out and was trying to pull my dress down. I rode back home with my friend and cried all the way there. I thanked him for saving me and he said no problem. My mother was still up and came to the door when my friend stopped the car in front of my parent's house.

"What happened? Where is Ezell? Why didn't he bring you back?" After telling my mother about her Prince Charming, she was surprised. She told me to go to bed and she planned to call his mother to let her know what her son tried to do to me. I felt that her dream of Ezell and me getting married had died on the backseat of his car. Thank you, Lord. I was thinking to myself that Paul and I had a good chance now. My mother said we would talk in the morning.

The next morning, Freddie called to see if I got the money, I told him that I was picking it up that day. I told him I would call him when I got it. After I hung up and I turned around; my mother was standing there looking puzzled. She asked me if Freddie knew I came to meet Ezell and that I might not be coming back. I said, "Yes". My mother said that he seemed like a good man and that I probably couldn't do badly by marrying him. She told me to go pack me and my son's clothes. My mother said that when we picked up the money, we would buy me a ticket back to Chicago. My mother told me, "If Freddie takes you back, marry him. I think he will be good to you and Victor." I asked, "What about Paul?" She replied, "What about Paul? You will never marry him while I am alive. You go to Chicago and marry Freddie; he has something to offer you!" I slammed out the room and threw myself on the bed and I cried until my eyes were swollen.

An hour later, my mother appeared and told me to start packing and that a bus was leaving West Helena at two o'clock that afternoon. True to his word, Freddie wired the money and I picked it up at the Piggly-Wiggly Grocery Store in West Helena. We picked up the money and purchased a ticket. By two fifteen, my son and I were sitting on the bus to Chicago. While Victor chatted on and on, I looked out the window and cried over what would never be...Paul and me; married and happy!

My son and I arrived in Chicago the first week of October after riding two buses for twelve hours. Freddie was standing there with a big smile as we exited the bus. He gave me a brief hug and picked Victor up. He was happy to meet Victor and the two of them just started talking like old friends. We left the bus station and the guys were holding hands. A few days later Freddie asked me if he could marry me. I shared it with my mother and she said, "Yes!" I asked her, "What about Paul?" She told me that I had found a good man, marry him and I would forget about Paul. Deep in my heart I knew that I would never forget Paul, who I loved dearly.

A week later, Freddie and I went downtown to the courthouse. Both of us were dressed in all black and Freddie had our gold wedding rings. There were no bells and no whistles. This was so different from the wedding Paul and I planned. After entering the courthouse, we were stopped by a preacher (he showed us his license) who said he could get our license and marry us for twenty dollars which would save us some time. He disappeared and when he returned, he found a corner and married us. He gave us a marriage license and we left. I felt nothing; not the excitement a woman feels on her wedding day. It was like I had just made an arrangement. Freddie was happy. I think he was happy because he had an instant family. He adored us. Of course, my mother was pleased with us getting married.

Since my rapes, I had never had sex, well a few had tried, but once I figured out that's what they wanted; I fought my way out of intercourse. I was agreeable when it came to hugs, but beyond hugs I couldn't go any further. I often wondered if I could have intercourse with Paul, but he never pushed the issue. He told me that it would be fine once we got married and that I didn't have to have sex even then. He would wait until I was ready. But that this was my wedding day, Freddie said he was moving us to his house after we left the courthouse. As we rode back to my aunt's house so he could move us, I pondered in my heart about coming face to face with my issue about sex.

Freddie was happy that we were married, and he made a point of flirting with me all day after the ceremony. My son was excited about his new father and followed him around the house. Freddie told me that Victor was now his son and he would fight anyone who said anything different. That made me happy because he and my son got along excellently.

Later that night I avoided going to bed for as long as I could. I was struggling with the thought that my new husband would expect me to perform my wifely duties that night. In my mind, I knew that's exactly what married people do. I was extremely apprehensive about what the night would bring.

It was horrible, it was terrible! I hated being touched in that manner. I hated that I was expected to kiss, to open myself to being violated. It felt like I was being assaulted all over again. I hated being married if I had to have sex. Freddie kept telling me that I was supposed to let my husband touch me and that it was alright for us to have sexual intercourse. That's how it was each time he touched me, unpleasant. I didn't like open mouth kissing. I know that I was a disappointment to my husband, but I didn't feel normal.

If you looked on the outside, it seemed that we had a perfect family. My husband worked hard and was an outstanding provider making sure that he gave me one hundred dollars every Friday to shop on Madison Street. I faithfully shopped every Friday and Saturday. It developed into my passion, shopping.

In many ways being married to Freddie was like still living with my parents all over again. I was not allowed to use profanity, wear revealing clothes, drink or smoke because I was a lady. Freddie made sure that I always carried myself like a young lady, but there still was one part of my marriage that was challenging, painful, and distasteful to me; the intimate part.

One year after our marriage my mother called me crying. She told me that she was standing at the stove cooking and my father came in the kitchen and stabbed her in her hip. My mother said that they were not arguing and he just stabbed her. She insisted that she was afraid to continue living in the house with my father. I reiterated all this to my husband and he said to tell her she could come live with us. So, I invited her to move here and bring all the children.

After sneaking, planning, and saving, my mother and six of my sisters and brothers arrived in Chicago a month later. My mother and the children lived with us for six months until we got her an apartment and Freddie surprised her with her very own car. She loved him for his kindness to her until she passed away March 19, 1998. He was kind to my family and he was kind to me until things changed.

After my mother came to Chicago, God began to do a work in both my mother and me, and we became closer. I started spending time talking to her and just trying to make sure she knew how sorry I was about all the pain I had caused her. I wanted to make her proud of me somehow. I began to realize that my mother had great desires for me. She wanted me to become a teacher which is why she tried to keep me away from Paul. She didn't want me to get trapped in a marriage with a bunch of babies with a man who was a tractor driver. But I didn't care about what Paul did for a living, he loved me. I felt safe with him, plus he made me feel like I mattered. I trusted him and could talk to Paul about anything. I never told him about "the secret." Afraid that he would explode and hurt my abusers; I remained silent. He was my most trusted friend and I had resented my mother for taking away the man I loved. Finally in the process of time, God gave me the strength to forgive my mother and the wisdom to understand that she was only doing what she thought was best for me. So, I moved forward by trying to be a good daughter, wife, and mother. I tried, but it was not easy.

Now that I was married to a man my mother approved of; I was not happy in my marriage. After two years of marriage, things changed. Our marriage became physically, emotionally, and psychologically abusive. My husband berated me; called me names, beat me, mentally abused me, and drank too much. I suffered in silence. I believe that he changed because I wasn't a real woman to him.

I became friends with a single, beautiful, young lady named Patricia, who had two children. She moved in the apartment above me. Her sister lived in the next building and we all became friends. Freddie loved playing cards with them, but he wouldn't let me play cards. This went on for a year.

Then one Saturday night, Freddie told me he was going upstairs to play cards. I said that was fine because I had some things I needed to do. Shortly after he arrived upstairs, I heard muffled sounds coming from the bedroom over mine. Suddenly, I heard Patricia calling Freddie's name out. I quickly ran upstairs and knocked on her door. Freddie screamed out and told me to go home. I asked him what he was doing. He said, "Having a good time." I heard them laughing as I went downstairs.

After that he made a habit of going upstairs most nights to play cards and I would hear the same kind of sounds. I realized that they were having sex. But what confused me was, it seemed like she enjoyed it. One day Patricia came downstairs and we talked. I quietly asked her was she having sex with Freddie. She gasped and then she said, "Yes!" Then I asked if she liked doing that and she replied, "Yes, don't you like him having sex with you?" I said, "No!" I just didn't understand how she could like having sex with my husband. I wasn't the least bit jealous.

Thinking to myself that if he liked having sex with her then he wouldn't bother me. She laughed and said I didn't know what I was missing. I didn't care that they liked having sex with each other as long as he didn't touch me. It would be years before I understood that my view of sex was directly connected to my sexual abuse. It had nothing to do with my husband but it was the result of what had happened to me. By now I was good at keeping secrets.

I hid the kind of marriage I had from my mother because she adored my husband. So, I began to suffer in silence. And since this marriage was a mess, I opened myself up to another avenue of friendship.

At work there was an older guy who befriended me and he always asked how I was and waited for a response. Guys were always telling me I was cute, but I knew that they were only interested in one thing. I only wanted attention and maybe a hug or two. It made me feel good to hear the guys say nice things to me when I was being called all kinds of names at home. So, I would seek the older guy out to talk when things got bad. Harry cared about me, but he kept his distance because I was married. We were friends for a long time. I shared so much of my unhappiness with him. He kept encouraging me to get my education, so I could take care of myself and my son on my own. My co-worker knew how much I wanted to teach and he believed in my vision. He was a great support system for me at that time because he didn't require sex or anything from me. He just wanted me to be happy and free. I knew that he secretly wanted to marry me, but I played it off because I didn't feel the same for him. I liked him as a friend.

By 1974 Freddie and I had been married for nearly four years when I had two life changing events: and I gave my life to Christ; I got saved January 11th and I got pregnant with my second child in September. These two life changing events changed my journey. I began to live for God and I enjoyed being in church again. On the other hand, my beautiful daughter, Freda Shvonne was born Tuesday, May 6, 1975 at 6:03 p.m. at Mt. Sinai Hospital on the Westside of Chicago. She was six pounds of joy to both of her parents. Her father and brother were so ecstatic at the new addition to the family. They both became Freda's protectors.

God had saved my soul and He had given me a beautiful daughter. I knew instinctively that I owed Him the debt of serving Him the rest of my life. Six months after getting saved, the Lord filled me with the Holy Spirit and I began to speak with new tongues. I had such a supernatural experience that I know it was all God. Also, I realized that the Father, Son, and Holy Spirit were real. I understood what it meant to be drunk in the Spirit. I had never had a drink, but this supernatural high was intoxicating; I loved it.

My world changed and my life changed. I was on fire for God. I was very excited about God and the things of God. I felt clean for the first time in my life. I loved the joy and the peace that filled me. I felt as if I was a new creature. The Bible says, **"Therefore, if anyone is in Christ, he is a new creation; old things have passed away; behold, all things have become new" (2 Corinthians 5:17).** After years of feeling worthless and powerless, I now was a brand new person. My heart and mind were filled with thanksgiving.

The Lord had come into my life and I was so happy except when I came home. It seemed that I was living in even more misery at home. My husband didn't understand my salvation. He did all he could to keep me away from the church. I felt that what he hated was his lack of control of me. Now I was Christ-driven. It didn't matter what he did or said. I had to go to church even if it meant being physically abused when I got home (which happened a lot). My faith and trust was in God. I set my face like a flint. I prayed that God would save my husband. I accepted God's call and plan for my life and I threw my life into ministry serving in different capacities my pastor assigned me with joy.

The Lord bought back the vision that He gave me when I was nine years old. It stayed on my mind. I would dream of preaching. I could hear myself preaching in my sleep. It was all in my belly. The Lord began to give me titles of sermons and the scriptures to go with them. Then my pastor started encouraging me to accept my call to preach. So shortly after I got filled with the Holy Spirit I preached my first message, *"Hell Is a Place You Don't Want to Go!"* I began to teach more and my confidence grew. I had a strong passion for prayer. Soon I was witnessing on the streets of Madison Avenue and preaching downtown on State Street.

God continually amazed me because He wanted to use me for His glory despite all I had gone through. However, I was being asked to preach here and there. My mother was so proud of me and I basked in her pride. All I ever wanted was for my mother to accept and love me. Now she did. I was so happy. I was still struggling with rejection and I wanted my mother's acceptance and approval. I prayed for healing every day, but healing from rejection eluded me.

Many days I wondered if salvation changed anything about my life. Did my life get better after my salvation? Yes and no, the part where I knew that God saved me, yes. In my personal life, no, it became horrible. But I kept pressing forward. I was an abused woman, so we don't talk about that in church. As abused women, many of us hide our pain in shame and fear. I learned how to mask the pain. I learned how to function and smile through the abuse until it was just unbelievable to family and friends that I was actually going through it.

In the midst of being in an abusive relationship, raising two children, working in a factory, Imperial Camera, I decided to quit my job and go to college full-time to pursue my teaching degree.

Realizing that many nights I would return home from church to a beating, I knew that returning to college, the beatings would intensify;

and they did. My husband slapped, punched, and even knocked me unconscious one day while attending school. Frequently, Freddie would tear up my homework and books or toss them in the toilet. My decision was met with more verbal and physical abuse. Despite the intense pressure at home, I completed my Associates of Arts Degree in Liberal Arts with honors in one year and graduated from Olive-Harvey College in June, 1979. In September, I then enrolled in Chicago State University to pursue a degree in Secondary English Teaching. After enduring eighteen months of verbal, emotional, physical abuse, hard work and burning the midnight oil along with working in ministry; I graduated with honors with my Bachelors of Arts Degree in English Literature and Secondary Teaching in June, 1981.

Freddie fought me completing my degree because he claimed that he was losing control of me. At the heart of most abuse, is control. My degree gave me power to obtain a career that would allow me to stand on my own feet when I made the exit from my abusive marriage. .

Listen, my husband was a great father, but we were not a great couple. We stayed together for our children. That is not the best thing for the mental health of your family. I stayed as long as I could. I left him after he informed me that he fathered a child that was born April, 1982 outside of our marriage. I left with my life, children, a few possessions, but I left with a good job. Many women don't make it out of abusive relationships.

As an educated and Christian woman, I was thoroughly embarrassed about being an abused woman. I have witnessed my mother's abuse by my father. I thought she and I were the only women I knew personally caught up in abusive relationships. In researching the topic, **The American Medical Association (AMA)** reports that *"A woman is beaten every 9 seconds. The FBI estimate 3-4 million women are battered each year in the U.S. Domestic Violence is the single greatest cause of injury to women. Women of all cultures, races, occupations, income levels, and ages are battered – by husbands, boyfriends, lovers and partners. White, Black and Hispanic women all incur about the same rates of violence committed by an intimate partner."* Domestic violence is real and to think that there are still many who don't believe that it exists is alarming to me. *The AMA further reports that, "Many women do leave abusive partners, more than 50%. Leaving a battering partner may be the most dangerous time in that relationship. Women are 70 times more likely to be killed in the two weeks after leaving than at any other time during the relationship. Social, economic, cultural, religious, or legal issues often keep battered women in an abusive relationship. Many women want the violence, not the relationship to end. They may take many steps to try to stop the abuse; leaving the home may be their last resort."* I have lived with and survived domestic violence; so grateful that God graced me to escape. Yet, there are still millions of women who suffer in silence everyday in the United States. Countless of these women can be found in the pews of many churches, bleeding. I was able to leave and embark further in my journey by embracing the vision God gave me for my life.

Notwithstanding, the enemy comes to *"kill, steal and destroy"* **(John 10:10b).** The enemy can even sleep next you nightly. The enemy chooses those close enough to you so he can use them to stop or derail you. He had his plan for my life and that plan was to continue to be used by him. Satan set traps for me to keep me needing someone or something other than God. Since I was vulnerable to relationships, he planted bad choices in my path to derail my assignment from God.

As a young preacher, I was not healed from rejection, shame, and fear, but I had an undeniable zeal for God and continued running for Him. Even though I was a young minister, I struggled in my vulnerabilities. Fighting through my issues, I gladly preached the gospel by praying and seeking God to help me continually. But Satan got angry with me by setting a snare for me. I was looking for love in all the wrong places.

Rejection, shame, and fear opened doors which are so difficult to keep shut. It does not matter what your age, socio-economic, educational, or ministry status you can experience the pain associated with rejection, shame and fear. Rejection causes you to seek your identity through what others think of you. Seeking approval from others is very destructive. I found out the hard way that seeking out the approval of others destroys your self-esteem and stunts your self-confidence. So when I couldn't get the approval and appreciation from my parents, I looked elsewhere.

Throughout my life, my one downfall has been that I have had an affinity for choosing the wrong man. For me, I define the wrong man as one who does not feel the same about me as I do for him. He does not have the God kind of love for me. Since I didn't love myself, I didn't know how to love a man back. Being unable to love has plagued me since my first love, Paul, walked out of my life in Chicago that hot summer evening. I have searched for the unconditional love he gave me in the relationships that followed ours. What I received in return was heartache and pain.

My dream has always been to be married to a wonderful man who loves me and who I could pour all the pinned-up love that was locked in the vault of my being. It seemed that I wanted marriage but I didn't open my eyes to see what God was showing me which was that the men I chose were not capable of loving me. They were unavailable emotionally and spiritually. I saw these men as "fixable". Knowing that they had serious problems didn't faze me, because I felt that my loving them could heal and change them. I was a fixer and an enabler in these relationships.

I tried to fix my relationship to Freddie by marrying and remarrying him twice over an eighteen year period without better results. A marriage without trust is a recipe for disaster. As an abused woman, trust was not a part of my makeup. So, our marriage failed before it began.

After Freddie and I divorced, I met a charming and handsome Christian man who had a zest for life. We met when I went out to dinner with some teachers from St. Willibrord High School where I taught English. I was attracted to him because he was tall, very dark, hilarious, and romantic. We dated for nearly two years and then we married in a very small marriage ceremony before Bible class January 11, 1984. I dreaded the wedding night and I was right; I hated it. It still seemed like rape to me. However, God blessed my womb the night we married and I became pregnant. Due to complications nearing the end of the pregnancy, doctors determined that they needed to induce my labor early. During delivery, I developed complications and the doctor informed my husband and mother that the baby and I were both in danger.

The doctor asked them which one of us he should try to save. Fortunately, the doctor was able to save both of us. My precious daughter, Ronneisha Corine was born on Wednesday, August 31, 1984 at 5:30 p.m. by cesarean section at Illinois Masonic Hospital on the North side of Chicago, Illinois. She weighed five pounds and twelve ounces and was so absolutely beautiful. When I bought her home her fifteen year old brother took her to his room and took care of her. She was his baby! Victor and Freda (who was now nine) spoiled Ronneisha to no end.

    While I carried Ronneisha in the womb, I was enthroned in an unhappy marriage, but I continued to preach the word of God. My faith and trust was in the God of my salvation. Going through hell didn't stop me from accepting my call or carrying out my assignment. Pregnant with my daughter, I preached and operated in ministry; sometimes having painful bruises under my clothes from my husband's beatings. I was able to persevere because I knew it was for purpose. Still, I knew that God had called Ronneisha to preach when she was in the womb. I knew that she was called to preach from my womb because preaching was in her blood. When the doctors discovered that the umbilical cord had wrapped around her neck three times, I knew Satan's assignment was to stop her from coming forth so she would not preach God's word. But the devil was a liar and still is!

    I had not healed from the cheating in my previous marriage when I found a pair of lady's panties five times smaller than what I wore in our bed as I made up our bed a few months later. My second husband told me that the panties came with the mattress when we purchased it from the furniture store. Of course, I did not believe him, but I stayed in the marriage. I did not stay in the marriage because I believed his lies; I stayed because of the rejection, shame and fear. I felt rejected because he chose another woman over me. Shame because I found myself in another troubled marriage and the fear of being middle-aged and alone was unbearable.

However, a few months later my husband asked me to pick him up from work by eight at night. Arriving at seven-thirty instead, I discovered my husband in his truck receiving oral sex from a lady of the night; I was devastated. The marriage was over that night and my husband left.

In 1986, after two years of marriage we separated and later divorced.. Here I was, alone and heart-broken with three children. I was struggling to provide for us. I continued to teach during the day and preach during the week and on Sundays as I had invitations.

Despite struggling with heartbreak, rejection, shame and fear, I continued to attend church and pressed through the pain even though I still was *"bleeding in the pews"*.

My children and I pulled together and we survived with God's help. For a two year period, money was an oddity and barely enough to cover the mortgage, car payment, insurance, light, gas, water, gas for the car, and day care for Ronneisha. There just was no money to purchase meat. We ate a lot of potatoes, rice, spaghetti, pinto beans, and vegetable soup.

One summer night, the doorbell rang and it was Freddie. We were so happy to see him. The children and I were just sitting down to dinner, so their father joined us. We had potato soup. Immediately, he asked about meat. The children all responded in unison, "We never eat meat!" We all enjoyed listening to Freddie as we laughed over dinner. It was great to have him here with us. He left shortly after dinner and he said he would be back tomorrow.

True to his word, Freddie came back the next night. He asked Victor to come downstairs to his car. When they came in the house, Freddie and Victor were carrying grocery bags filled with meat: steaks, pot roasts, pork chops, chickens, turkey legs, bacon, sausages, cold cuts, hot dogs, and ground beef. The children were so happy. Freddie told me that from now on, he would buy us all the groceries we needed. He stepped up and helped us out tremendously. When he asked me four months later to get married so he could help me, I accepted his proposal. We were married in November 1988. Nothing had changed for me; my view of being intimate was the same. We made an agreement that I didn't have to sleep with him. My husband only married me to help me and to be with our children. This was fine with me. It was a delicate arrangement.

Not understanding that I was in the midst of a familiar cycle, I had remarried Freddie again for the wrong reasons. Actually, both of us married each other for all the wrong reasons. I married him for security and he married me to be with his children, but those reasons were not strong enough to build a strong foundation for marriage. We were unhappy. Afterwards, Freddie resumed his relationship with a former girlfriend; we separated and divorced several months later. We wholeheartedly agreed and committed to being successful and loving parents to our three children even though our marriage did not work. That part of relationship worked very well.

The cycle continued to spin. In September, 1989 I started a new teacher's position at a troubled high school in the inner city in Chicago. In 1990 I met Leonidas Howard who was a tall, dark, distinguished and intelligent man who had a degree in Social Services who had a passion for helping young men. He was a soft spoken, kind, and gentle man. We started dating the beginning of 1991. I felt that he came into my life at the right time. We would talk for hours and I just loved talking to him. Leonidas fell in love with my pastor and church. His heart was so open to the teaching as he had been raised Catholic. He gave his life to Jesus shortly afterward. After a brief courtship, we married. Leonidas was patient with me and he let me know that there was no rush to do anything. He waited patiently for me and that made me love him so much. When that time came, it was different; a good different!

We spent thirteen wonderful years together. My children grew to love him and his sons accepted me as their father's wife. We had fun and we continued dating each other after we married. Leonidas and I worked together and we rode to and from work daily for thirteen years. We had a very deep love for each other. Unlike my love for Paul, the love I had for Leonidas was a mature love. With me being thirty-seven and his being thirty-five, we had lived a lot of life since being teenagers. The love I had for Paul was a sweet, tender and precious love of a starry eyed eighteen year old. In my heart, I knew that I would always love Paul because he had the honor of being my first love. But now as a full grown woman I had the experience of being in love with a wonderful man.

Leonidas and I worked together, exercised, dealt with children, bills, ministry, deaths of our parents, obstacles, trials, and tribulations, but at the end of the day; we had each other's love. Our love was strong and for real. We were always there for each other.

My husband and I never thought anything would separate us, but it did. We hit a major bump in our relationship in September of 2001 that we could not agree on at all. I gave him thirty days to make his choice. He chose the opposite of what I wanted. I made a decision to leave and I realized later that I should have given him another chance. I should have stood by my husband's decision, but because I was more concerned about pleasing people, I focused on my reputation. I didn't understand that my fear of being rejected by some people that I held in high esteem caused me to do anything to be seen by them in a certain. I was more concerned about what they thought of me than I was about my husband. What I did, in fact, was to reject my husband who really loved me. I hurt him. That's what rejected people do; they reject people. Hurting people hurt people.

My failure was that I didn't stand up for my husband. He

deserved a wife who should have stayed through the storm, but I got out the boat (our relationship). He taught me what it meant for a man to love a woman. He took care of me when I had surgery, he flew to Arkansas to be with me every chance he got while I sat by my mother's bed for 40 days before she passed away, he defended me countless times at school from co-workers and students who crossed the line; and he gave me his heart and best self he had ever been. But the one time, he needed me to stand with him, I left him.

Mind you, Leonidas was a good man, good husband, and good father. He loved my children like he loved his sons. He made countless sacrifices for them as I did. We were a great team. This man supported me at home, at work and in ministry. He allowed me the space to purse my goals even going back to school to earn my third college degree, a Master's of Arts Degree in English Literature which took me ten years to complete. The day I graduated he cried because he was so proud of me.

My leaving Leonidas was devastating and destructive to both of us which led us down paths of never returning to each other. After thirteen years, we were divorced. I was heartbroken for two years after our divorce and I made up my mind that I would never ever love again. I decided I would never have a romantic love for another man.

One of the most amazing things about my marriage to Leonidas is that when I began my journey of healing and deliverance from sexual, emotional and physical abuse in 1996, he encouraged me through the process, wiped away tears and listened to every new uncovered painful event. I am so thankful for all he did to assist me in my ongoing discovery and healing. I will always love him for this. Additionally, he taught me by showing me what a man loving a woman looked like. Thank you, Leonidas.

The cycle continued and two years later I met an ordained Elder who had an awesome knowledge of the scriptures. I was just excited that this man had such a command of the scriptures and that is what drew me to him. It didn't matter that he was a big man, dark, and not that tall. The Elder was very old-fashioned and romantic; he would send me flowers, candy, and cards. He showed a lot of interest in me. Finally, he proposed to me and gave me a beautiful diamond ring. I was thrilled at his romantic gesture. I accepted his proposal and felt we would do well in ministry together because I knew God had prepared me to be a Pastor. Eight months later, we married in a wonderful wedding ceremony. It was a beautiful wedding. After the reception, we rode to our honeymoon in a beautiful silver Rolls Royce. Our honeymoon was a disaster. Nothing was consummated. As a matter of fact, we never consummated our marriage.

Then in December 2005, I was commissioned along with my husband to start a prayer cell in my home by our Senior Pastor & Overseer, Apostle Dozier. Despite the intimate side of our relationship failing, we agreed to start the prayer cell in our home. We launched the prayer cell out of our home with twelve people the first week of February, 2006. The Lord blessed our prayer cell to grow to the point that we ran out of space in our home. In June, Apostle Dozier released me to look for a facility and God blessed us to find space in a funeral home where there was seating for three hundred people. We moved into the build with fifty people. In a year, we had one hundred and fifty members.

In late August, my husband informed me that his lady friend that he had been seeing for fifteen years was near death from cancer. He sobbed all that night telling me about their relationship and how much he loved her. I asked him if he was in love with her, he said, "Yes!" Next, I asked if their relationship was sexual, he said, "Yes!" I was stunned by his revelation. I was shocked. I wasn't extremely mad at him; I was horrified. I asked him why he married me. He told me that he married me because he liked the status I had as a Chicago Public School teacher, an ordained Elder in my church, had a nice suburban home, and that I drove a brand new Lexus. He said, "What man could pass up all of that?" I thanked him for telling me the truth finally, but I was mortified by his graphic admission.

His girlfriend died quietly early the next morning. Of course, he felt he had to go be with the family when the hospital requested that the family come immediately to the hospital. When he returned early the next morning he told me that the family wanted him to do her funeral. What he said next floored me. He said, "I am going to do her funeral and I want you to be the Mistress of Ceremonies for the program." After staring at him like he had lost his mind, I told him, "No!"

Six days later, he left for the funeral. I had to have a witness because I could not believe the current situation in which I found myself. I decided to go to the funeral. My oldest daughter, Freda, told me I could not go alone; so she said that she was going with me. I also picked up my best friend, Elder Betty, and his ex-wife, Paula; and we went to the funeral. The place was packed, but we managed to find four seats toward the back. There was my husband, standing in the pulpit, telling the mourners about how much he loved this woman who he thought he would marry someday. He was strutting like a peacock until he looked in the back and saw us. I stood up so he could clearly see me and we left. When he came home he was furious that I failed to come and do as he requested. I told him that it was over and to move out of my house. He refused. I made him a room next door. I moved him and his belongings out of my room and into the empty bedroom next door.

Despite living through another very public breakup, it was during this time that I was appointed as the Elder in Charge (EIC) of Power & Light West Christian Center in June 2006. I worked tirelessly launching the new ministry as I was coming to terms with leaving my marriage. We lived separately all summer. I made plans to leave and I put my home on the market for sale.

On September 30, I moved. In December I received divorce papers from my husband. I wasn't in love with him but I had only been attracted to the spiritual side of him. Our marriage couldn't stand on the foundation of all that he had done to me. I felt that my husband betrayed me like others in my life had done. Betrayal is extremely painful to a person who has suffered from it several times and by people close to them. Betrayal by any person is painful, but betrayal by a friend cuts deep wounding the soul. We expect that betrayal can come from those on the outside, but what do you do when it comes from among your own circle, your trusted few, your parents, or spouse? What do you do when people who say they love you, but they hurt you and often? It starts with you forgiving those who betrayed you, but it is a process. You can do it if you want to be emotionally healthy. So I could not hold anything against my husband's girlfriend. First, she had died, and second, I did not make vows with her.

I didn't hate or blame the woman. I blamed myself for settling for this man because I didn't want to be alone. Until God heals you, what you will do is repeat your mistakes of the past like I did.

Eventually, the Elder and I were divorced two months later. I was glad to be delivered from this non-marriage and I determined to focus on ministry.

One thing about a cycle, it doesn't stop; it repeats itself. In 2003,

I had met man while he was living in California,. I chose not to develop a relationship with him, but three years later he contacted me after he moved back to Kenosha, Wisconsin; I was divorced by this time. I invited him down to church. I had just gone through a divorce and I wasn't looking for a relationship.

This guy was five feet-seven inches, medium built, brown shinned with a bubbly personality. He was very outgoing and had degrees in Computer Programming and Business Management. After a few months of attending my ministry; he joined. He was an asset to our very young ministry because he had knowledge about the business end of ministry. He really loved the church and would drive an hour from Wisconsin each week to attend service. We talked a lot and I knew he liked me but I kept it on a spiritual basis. He kept telling me I was his wife. I saw this possible marriage as being a great merger and that we could do a lot for God together. He would work behind the scenes in ministry. We both had previous marriages and we did not want to divorce again and that was a plus for me.

Two years later, he proposed. We were married in a very small ceremony in February 2008. There were problems in the marriage, but I was determined to stay in what I considered my last marriage. It had been seven years since I had been intimate; but I still had issues with intimacy. We were married for four years and the problems magnified over time. He and I were miserable living separate lives under the same roof. After numerous conversations, we both agreed we deserved better than this. More shame enveloped me because here I was in another broken marriage. I tried to make it work but it was to no avail. During the marriage, I was trying to balance a troubled marriage, a growing family, new ministry, and demanding job. I was humiliated to admit that I had failed at marriage again. I was ashamed because of the failures of all my marriages. I was disappointed that our business partnership wasn't strong enough to make the marriage work.

Marriage is about trust, commitment, and love, and when you are a broken individual there is a battle to trust, commit and love. So, the relationship is doomed. You can have a beautiful wedding and reception, but you have to live with the person after the honeymoon and that is when it gets real. That is when you see who you have married and they see who they have married. Without a doubt, my husband was not a bad person; things were stacked against us when we married.

We amicably divorced in 2012 after four years of marriage. We chose to remain friends, even now. I thank God for us committing to being friends. This friendship would be important in the days ahead. After our divorce, my mindset was: I tried marriage, it didn't work now let me do what I know I am proficient at, ministry. I set my face to do kingdom business. I moved on with God. And it was well with my soul.

There's an old saying that says, "Straight, no chaser" that epitomizes all of what I have shared in this chapter. I am giving you the straight truth without anything added because it's my story and I want to help someone. If by sharing my truth, I can help free another person who is *"bleeding in the pews"* then it's worth it for me. If I can help the women, men and children trapped in a cycle of emotional, physical, and sexual abuse, and then it is worth all of what I am sharing and what I have experienced.

I would have never been able to share the truth of my numerous marriages before I got delivered. I would have been too ashamed. I often tell people as I minister that once you get delivered you can tell the truth. As I write this, I know some of you are counting my husbands, but go ahead and count. My purpose is to share how I was caught up in a cycle in looking for love in relationships with men instead of looking to God.

No matter who tried to help me spiritually, I didn't listen. I kept getting married because I thought having a man would solve all my problems. Marriage could never heal the emotional, physical, and sexual scars I had. I had been damaged in every way possible and I needed healing. To tell my story now means only one thing, I am healed. My motive behind this book is to help someone else obtain their deliverance. I also want to encourage others who have fallen into a dangerous cycle of relationships that deliverance is available to you because you are reading my book and there is deliverance for you written on the pages of my life. My transparency is with divine purpose.

If my suffering can help one person then this book is not in vain!

How did God heal me? What was the process He used to being wholeness in my life? God began another part of my journey to healing when my best friend asked me a starling question.

I had to take a more in-depth look at my life when my best friend, Elder Betty, asked me a question that challenged me to the core. The question, "Why do you think you always marry men who hurt you?" This question haunted me to my core and it sent me in search of an answer which caused me to hurt anew but in a good way. It propelled me on my journey toward healing. I got angry with my friend because she had been married to the same man for over thirty years and she couldn't understand my pain. How dare she challenge me? I foolishly told myself that at least I was married.

For over forty years, I never slept with a man I wasn't married to since I had been saved. That was my immature boast. Realizing finally that without pain there can be no growth. Out of this new pain, I discovered the pieces to the puzzle of my life over the next few years. I had to drop to my knees and seek God for the answer instead of wasting time being angry with the wrong person.

Many times our lives are like broken puzzles with missing pieces. These pieces are scattered on the many roads we have traveled during our lives. In my quest to connect the pieces of my life, I have come full circle and have finally found the pieces that I have searched for all my life.

Although, I have made questionable choices in the men that I have married; having had several marriages have brought me great shame and humiliation. Being married to an alcoholic, serial cheater, drug user, thug, sexual deviant, and cyber cheater caused me great shame and heartache. Often I thought something was wrong with me instead of realizing that I needed emotional, physical and sexual healing. I was a broken and an abused woman using relationships to be whole. I was too broken to have a healthy marriage. It took a lifetime of pain to grasp this revelation.

Looking back over the marriages I have had, I reflect back to my honeymoons; I realized that they were short-lived after waking up to the reality that they could not fill the big hole in my being. I feel that the men I married were looking for something different from what I was seeking. My expectations were minimized due of my low opinion of myself. I was delighted and honored that these men would take me as their wives, but didn't expect what I got in return. It was all because I didn't understand my worth. When you deal with rejection, it is challenging to believe that you are worth much; or that you are valuable.

I made the mistake of not seeing my worth and therefore, I lowered my standards just to have a man in my life. Lowering your standards causes you to accept crumbs in a relationship. Sometimes you are the only person in the relationship because the other person does not view you as you view them. Like Leah in Genesis, she accepted a relationship with Jacob as his second wife when she knew he was in love with her sister Rachel and she continually conceived children with him in hopes that he would finally love her. The author of Genesis writes that, **"When the Lord saw that Leah was unloved, He opened her womb; but Rachel was barren. ³² So Leah conceived and bore a son, and she called his name Reuben; for she said, "The Lord has surely looked on my affliction. Now therefore, my husband will love me" (Genesis 29:31-32).** I also settled in past relationships just to say I had a man. If I was alone, I had to deal with the recriminations from the enemy; rejection, shame and fear. Thinking that the presence of a husband in my bed could keep away the memories, pain, shame and fear was fruitless. It did not work because the stain of it all was imprinted in my mind, body and spirit. After marrying me, these men rejected me and my love. I was now ashamed because I had married again and the marriage failed. Finally, I battled the fear of being by myself. Growing older alone is frightening to some women, especially to me because that is not the dream I had for my personal life.

The Bible gives us hope in that God says, "I will never leave or forsake you." This portion of scripture provides comfort to our mind, but what we really want In reality is another person to share our daily lives with on earth. There is where the problem is that God is not enough for us. So we tell ourselves that God didn't make us to be alone. Therefore, we deceive ourselves and set ourselves up for loneliness by believing we cannot live alone. The older we become, the thought of being alone for the rest of our lives is even more devastating in our minds. I had to examine my relationship with God and see if He was the center of my life or if I was making a relationship with a man a higher priority. As we look deep, sometimes what God shows us brings more pain. Illumination does bring revelation. We need revelation to move us closer to our deliverance and healing.

After finding that there was more damage done to me by being in these relationships, I came to the understanding that I needed inner healing for the sexual, emotional, and physical abuse I had suffered. Much of the painful memories of my abuse were buried in my subconscious and God only revealed them in pieces similar to pieces of puzzle at various times when He saw that I could handle the revelation. The things I had buried affected my ability to trust and develop intimate or close relationships with men and even women because I erected walls around my heart and life. I was bleeding profusely because I was definitely *"bleeding in the pews"* each week as I attended the weekly services in my church. The bleeding was a direct result of the suffering I had endured during my entire life.

Remember, until you deal with your wounds, you will never experience the freedom to love or receive love or even enjoy the physical aspect of an intimate relationship within the marriage. Despite being a woman heavily involved in ministry, it didn't heal my wounds. I was merely able to avoid the wounds by throwing myself in ministry and wearing a spiritual mask which I did not even realize I had. It is so easy to see what another person's problems are and so difficult to see your own problems.. I was able to minister to the pain of others but, I knew I had my own problems. I had to face my past, traumas, and pain because they were not going anywhere until I allowed God to truly come into my life and dig me out of the pit that I had buried myself in my entire life. Even though I could, pray, teach and preach, I was a woman bleeding in the pews until I opened myself up to trust in the True Healer of my damaged emotions.

Corine H. Stone

CHAPTER 9
MY JOURNEY TO DELIVERANCE AND HEALING

"The Spirit of the LORD is upon Me, Because He has anointed Me To preach the gospel to the poor; He has sent Me to heal the brokenhearted, To proclaim liberty to the captives And recovery of sight to the blind, To set at liberty those who are oppressed; 19 To proclaim the acceptable year of the LORD."(Luke 4:18-19)

When there are deeply, painful traumas that we have experienced in our past, they will have a profound effect upon our lives. The traumas will cause horrible emotional scars that are layered. Each trauma in your life causes another layer of pain that is stacked on top of the last trauma. I call this the *"pancake effect"*, a stacking of the pain on top of pain. Over the years, if healing hasn't occurred, the stack of pancakes becomes hard as rock. For me, being rejected, molested, raped, emotionally, psychologically and physically abused damaged my mind, soul and spirit and each caused a stacking of the pain that became hardened over the years like a stack of rock hard pancakes!

Although God saved me at twenty, called me to preach, and used me for His glory, I was damaged emotionally and this affected every relationship I had. My past had affected how I viewed everyone, myself, and even God. I had to honestly look at my life and the stream of broken relationships that lay in my past. Notwithstanding, I had managed to raise my children, graduate from college with three degrees with honors, minister locally, nationally and even internationally; but I realized that there was some tender areas in my life that needed some work.

I needed inner healing. What then is "inner healing"? According to David Seamands, he explains in his study, **Healing for Damaged Emotions** states that, *"In the process of inner healing, Jesus uncovers those painful memories piece by piece; like an onion with the layers being peeled away one at a time. "New birth", being "born again" or an "infilling by the Holy Spirit" will not always automatically heal these areas. Prayer, discipline and willpower alone will not bring us to that peaceful place. A special kind of healing is needed– unlearning ways of acting based on emotional trauma and scars and relearning a new way of thinking and acting. Once we become aware of wanting a more intimate relationship with Jesus and begin to trust Jesus more we are able to open our hearts to healing and allow His love to more deeply penetrate our hearts."* Getting saved, filled with the Holy Ghost, teaching and preaching did not heal me on the inside. It took years and years to even understand that I had inward wounds. So God sent me help!

Way back in 1986, God had sent a man and woman of God into my life who loved me to life by speaking life into me. These leaders saw the good in me before I did; and constantly told me that I was intelligent, beautiful and anointed, but I could not receive it. They taught me that if I didn't have a revelation of who I was, I would never receive what they said to me because there were some blockages due to damaged emotions that prevented me from seeing my true self.

Apostle Benny L. & Prophetess Gerry Dozier labored with me for ten years until God gave them the strategy that would eventually set me free. The Bible says, **"And you shall know the truth, and the truth shall make you free" (John 8:32).** God used my senior pastors to transform my life because they pointed me toward the truth. Apostle Benny L. Dozier prayed for me and pushed me toward my journey of deliverance and healing. He saw my heart and the anointing on my life, but he also felt that my life had some areas of disarray even though my gift was working, my lifestyle needed rescuing. I will forever thank them for all they have done for me.

I did not realize that until I started the journey of healing that God planted a hedge around my mind by taking the "secrets" and burying them deep in my sub-couscous; and shielding my mind from the enemy. Satan wanted my mind as well as my life! John 10:10 says that, **"The thief does not come except to steal, and to kill, and to destroy. I have come that they may have life, and that they may have it more abundantly."** My greatest enemy (the thief) wanted to steal what God had put inside of me, kill the assignment on my life and destroy my life by any means necessary! I was tortured mentally most of my life with feelings of worthlessness, despair and suicide. Death was constantly in my mind bringing with it thoughts of killing myself because I did not matter to anyone. I felt that I was an outcast who didn't deserve to live. Never did I understand as a child or an adult my true worth as a person. The enemy tried to drag me in a pit deep enough that I would want to be buried there. But God!

My Senior Pastor, Apostle Dozier realized that there were some things going on in my life that I needed to deal with and God revealed this strategy to him for me to develop and teach an abuse class. He knew that any topic I taught I would seek the Lord and study. He prayed that God would bring forth healing in my life through this teaching. Because of God's love, He protected me by keeping some of my childhood abuse hidden from me. In the process of time, God began to reveal (uncover) the things that were hidden, so I could began my journey to healing as I began to study for a teaching assignment on "Sexual Abuse". Thank you, Lord for Your protection.

The details of my abuse were painful and liberating as I addressed the issues and effects of sexual abuse while teaching Sunday Morning Life Class. God led me to teach from a book by Joyce Meyers, **Beauty for Ashes: Receiving Emotional Healing**, about her survival and healing from being sexually abused by her father. It was liberating to know that I was not the only woman who had been sexually abused by their father.

Similarly, like Meyers I had difficulty in maintaining intimate relationships in my personal life. Meyers' book helped me to admit the truth about my abuse and caused me to face the shame that I had tried to cover up all my life. My shame centered on my having been molested, raped and my failed relationships. It cut deeply. I was ashamed to the point that I believed if people knew those things about me, they would hate me. Therefore, it was difficult to maintain relationships for me.

An abused person has numerous challenges dealing with relationships and trust. Seamands further states that, *"When we find difficulty in relationships, difficulty with sinful responses, an inability to find peace or an inability to have a closer relationship with Jesus Christ, then inner healing will be the easiest way to heal the areas of our lives that are producing the turmoil"* (Healing). Admitting that I had difficulties with my relationships, finding peace and even getting closer to God was very challenging to me in every sense of the word.

Healing begins in the place of truth. You have to be honest with yourself. If you continue to lie to yourself, inner healing will never be your portion. The Bible says that, **"If we confess our sins, He is faithful and just to forgive us our sins and to cleanse us from all unrighteousness" (1 John 1:9).** I had to confess (admit) my problems and sins to myself and God to facilitate my inner healing process. *"If you believe in the saving grace of Jesus death on the cross and in the power* of the Holy Spirit He sent to us after His death, then you can know that He can heal us emotionally, physically, and spiritually. Out of the gifts of the Holy Spirit comes the gift of inner healing. When Jesus healed, he healed not only physical ills but also spiritual and emotional ills. Inner healing deals mainly with restoring our emotional and spiritual health. It is not counseling or psychiatric care although some counselors also use inner healing. Many times with inner healing people are healed physically" (Seamands). Finally, I came to the realization that Jesus was the only One who could reverse the damage done and heal me completely.

When you are caught up in cycles of abuse it is so difficult to face or even see what you are caught up in cycles of being in relationship after relationship with the same results. A cycle is defined as, *"a set of events or actions that happen again and again in the same order; a repeating series of events or actions; any complete round or series of occurrences that repeats or is repeated; it is circular"* (Webster). Through teaching my abuse class, I finally understood that after my first marriage ended, I kept marrying the same kind of man who did not see my worth. How could he see it when I saw no value in myself? However, after having been saved and preaching I had a deep conviction about being married because I did not want to commit fornication. Rather than being alone, I married. So, I ended up with a "pancake effect" by piling more pain on top of the pain in my first, second, third, and fourth relationships. My relationships would never get better until I did the work needed and thus getting the inner healing that I wanted.

There I was de-valuing myself to the point that I lost my true identity. My freedom was lost, my self-worth eroded and what was left was only a shell of the person God meant me to be. I can admit that I have wasted much time in this perpetual cycle of loving men who could never love me.

I had to come face to face with myself after losing the second man I loved when we were divorced after thirteen years of marriage. What God showed me was not a pretty picture. I lost the man I loved because I was a people pleaser. I was more interested in what some people thought of me, thereby, causing me to lose my marriage. It was entirely my fault because I should have stood up for my husband. But when you deal with rejection, you always seek the approval of man. You cannot get your identity from a relationship or friendship. Realizing that the abuse class had bought forth some healing, but I knew then I still had more healing to obtain. I was feeling rejected, dejected, ashamed and fearful. I was feeling lost. What I feared had come upon me; I was alone! Alone was the best season for me because I had to find out who I was. I had to learn some hard truths about myself.

After my divorce in 2003, I entered a new season in my life and I wanted to learn how to love myself. I had learned so much about myself after teaching my Abuse Class and I found that I was anointed, compassionate, intelligent, romantic, affectionate, but lonely. So I needed to be true to who I am. I asked myself, "Who am I? Why have I failed so in my quest to get what I want in life?" No one understands me or why I want what I want. I tell people that I am happy and fulfilled all the time, but on the inside only God and I know the truth. I was still basing my identity on what people thought about me. It was time for me to change. I made a better decision for moving forward in God. I had to transform my mind by renewing it through the Word of God. My mindset needed changing.

As long as I thought little of myself, I would continue to make the same choices and get the same results. It didn't matter that I was an ordained minister. The problem was I was not yielded to God in some areas of my personal life especially in the area of relationships. I had not submitted myself totally to God or let alone anyone else. I most definitely didn't trust anyone. No one could advise me about my relationships. I rejected counsel in that area. Rejected people reject also.

Purposefully, I stopped giving away pieces of myself so that I could be whole. I always give and give and others take and take. I wanted to stop feeling that I am not worth anyone's love. I always attempted to purchase what I wanted. I stooped and stooped. Pretty soon I was so low until my face was level to the ground. I wanted to stand up and embrace the woman that God made me to be. I am a good woman and great woman. I have survived things that have killed others. I know that there is purpose in my pain. There is a purpose in my failures which has made me human. I really feel for people when they suffer and what they are going through because I have undergone great suffering in my life. If they hurt I want to be there. Is this a way of escaping my own pain?

How did God heal me? First, I had to know I needed healing. Second, I had to forgive those who had hurt me. Third, I had to be open to how God wanted to heal me. Fourth, I had to be willing to follow simple instructions. Fifth, I had to humble myself to God and the people God assigned to help me. You too can be healed with these simple steps. If it worked for me; these steps will work for you. I have learned that I didn't have to get my education from the University of Hard Knocks. The choice was all mines.

I knew that I needed healing and teaching my Abuse Class confirmed my decision to obtain healing because I needed it. I became transparent in the reality of my pain. I stripped my prideful clothing off and I exposed all of what happened to me. God created an atmosphere in my environment where I was safe and accepted.

In my process, I traveled on the road to healing next began with active decision to forgive those who had abused and hurt me. It was a lesson I had learned when I first came to Christ. How could I expect God to forgive me when I wouldn't forgive those who had wronged me? The first person I forgave was my father. I prayed and prayed not to hate my father. I constantly asked God to help me forgive him and my rapists because they couldn't have known exactly what they did to me. They did not have a clue about the depth of pain they caused me.

It has always been my heart's desire not to become a bitter, hateful, and spiteful woman because of what I have suffered. This was a constant and daily prayer. None of my abusers asked me to forgive them and neither did they ever apologize. It was the power of God that helped to forgive them. My remaining problem stemmed from the fact that I couldn't forgive myself.

God confirmed to me that I had forgiven my father when he had a heart attack and stroke after he retired in 1989. I stood by his hospital bed and pleaded with God to let him live. All I knew is that I wanted him to live. For thirteen years my father had to be cared for and I was in charge of his care. I cared for him even after he developed Alzheimer's. I give God the praise because I knew that I loved my father and I wanted him to have the best care. I couldn't forgive him on my own, but God gave me the strength to forgive him. Then God gave me a test to confirm it and I passed. I took care of my father until he passed away September, 2003. Please, those of you who are reading this book, know that you can forgive even the worst people who hurt you.

Healing is similar to peeling an onion; it is one layer at a time. Healing will come in layers over time. Many times it takes years to forgive and get healed. Forgiving those who abused you is the first layer of healing. There will be no healing without forgiveness first. God taught me to forgive those who had hurt me. Many times we wait for those who hurt us to come back and apologize, but most of the time that never happens. So when we hold unforgiveness in our hearts toward someone, we are the ones who remain in bondage. But when we forgive, we open the door for deliverance. Forget about what you think you deserve. Yes, we deserve people to acknowledge their wrongs done to us. Let it go. Cast it on Jesus. Therefore, I forgave my parents, my abusers, and finally, I forgave Corine! I forgave myself. This was my greatest hurdle forgiving myself. I gave up my right to be right!! This surrender catapulted me to another level of freedom and deliverance.

Did I make poor choices after my journey began? Yes I did. Did I make mistakes, yes, I did make more. Marry again, yes I did. Divorce again, yes I did. Did I learn, all I can say is, "Yes, I did?" Did it come at a great cost, yes! What did it cost me? When I received my bill for my mistakes; it was more than I wanted to pay. It exhausted and bankrupted me. That's the best place for healing. This is when you reach in your bag and nothing is there.

My next step in my healing process took me over hills and down through valleys, but after thirteen years, I saw the door that had been standing before me for thirteen years. Jesus said, *"Behold, I stand at the door and knock. If anyone hears My voice and opens the door, I will come in to him and dine with him, and he with Me" (Revelations 3:20).* Our Savior loves us and He wants to heal us. We just have to want to be healed. I was ready now. ***"He heals the brokenhearted and binds up their wounds" (Psalms 147:3).*** What does it mean to be healed? To be healed means, *"to make sound or whole; to cause an undesirable condition to be overcome; mend, patch up, restore to original purity or integrity, cure, fix, mend, and rehabilitate" (Webster).* I needed God to heal me, make me whole again, and patch up all the holes in my traumatized soul. Like Humpty Dumpy, I needed to be put together again.

In order to obtain healing, there has to be knowledge of what you need to be healed and how God wants to heal you. Regardless, you will never be healed without the knowledge of what you need healing. I always knew that my father and I had a "relationship" and I knew that I had been raped twice on the same day. I knew about these incidents, but I never allowed myself to focus on them. I swept them under the rug of my subconscious because they were painful and embarrassing which bought much shame to my being. But I had to be open to this part of the process. I had to be open to dealing with the pain God's way and not mine's.

God allowed the details of the incidents to surface along with the pain, hurt, feelings of helplessness, hopelessness, rejection, shame and fear. I began to experience all the emotional ravages of being molested and raped. I felt the filth, uncleanliness, pain and disappointment. I was like every woman who dreamed of the knight on the white horse who would fall in love with me and sweep me off my feet. My knight would propose, marry me and whisk me off on a romantic honeymoon. But how could I ever wear the white gown? The recriminations enveloped me as I taught my class.

I had to face it, but God was with me. In 1995, God called me to be a Pastor. I knew healing was important because God called me to pastor people who needed a shepherd to love them. God spoke to several times during prayer that year. I had no response. Often I would ask God, "Why me?" But He never stopped calling me.

Finally, one Sunday after service, the power of God overshadowed me; I fell in the floor of the sanctuary and heard Him said to me, *"I have called you this day to preach healing and deliverance through my word to people that I will give you. They will need a shepherd to comfort them in love and the word. I have called you to pastor. You will love them supernaturally and nurture them to maturity. I will give you souls who will cry out for all that I have placed in you...but fear not! What I will do for you; you will do for them by giving them love and deliverance through the ministry I have placed inside of you. They will be delivered through the power of My love. Your ministry will be a ministry of love and deliverance."* After I stood up, I embraced what God said, but I pondered it in my heart because I felt unworthy due to all the mistakes and all the traumas I had experienced. Healing became my immediate quest. How did God heal me? What steps did God use to heal me? First, He healed me through the revelation of His word.

Illumination & Revelation

My absolute decision to teach an abuse class was the outward proof that I was ready to be healed. God began to deal with me concerning the Word of God concerning healing and deliverance. In the Bible the Prophet Isaiah, declares that, *"He is despised and rejected by men, a Man of sorrows and acquainted with grief. And we hid, as it were, our faces from Him; He was despised, and we did not esteem Him.[4] Surely He has borne our griefs. And carried our sorrows; yet we esteemed Him stricken, smitten by God, and afflicted. [5] But He was wounded for our transgressions, He was bruised for our iniquities; the chastisement for our peace was upon Him, And by His stripes we are healed" (Isaiah 53:3-5).* I have read these scriptures and I thought they were good verses and I have even preached these very verses; but as I began my journey to wholeness, God breathed on this word and it became alive to me.

The verses brought illumination which birthed the revelation that Jesus had carried my pain, grief, sorrow, humiliation, rejection, shame and fear to the cross! He bore all this turmoil I was carrying and if I had truly accepted the Lord, I could do an exchange with my Savior without cost. Hallelujah!!! My God, glory to the Most High God song in my heart. Just learning through God's word that Jesus wanted me to be healed and willingly gave His life for my healing opened the door of my understanding. He was wounded for me. He bore my rejection, molestation, rapes, shame, and fear on the cross with Him.

We can carry our Bibles and even read the scriptures, but until you open your heart to God the revelation of His word will remain hidden. As I opened my heart and submitted my will and way to Jesus, God illuminated the word and I received clarity and revelation. I gained access to my deliverance and healing. In the final steps in my process, I had to learn how to follow precise instructions and humble myself to who God was using to help bring deliverance and healing in my life. I could not choose the how or who in my healing process.

How great God is towards me? I began to believe that I was worthy of being healed and that I could be healed. I was worthy, I was so worthy because now I could exchange all the hurt, all the pain, all the suffering, all the rejection, all the shame, and all the fear because Jesus already carried my past and mistakes to the cross and I didn't have to carry the weight or the stain of it any longer. Thank You, Lord God!! How did God heal me? He healed me through His unwavering love.

LOVE

The Word of God was unlocked for me during this period. I perceived the reality of God's love. I delved into the scriptures I had preached on before many times. Another great scripture that I read and quoted so many times was, **"For God so loved the world that He gave**

His only begotten Son, that whoever believes in Him should not perish but have everlasting life. ¹⁷ For God did not send His Son into the world to condemn the world, but that the world through Him might be saved" (John 3:16-17). Since I was teaching high school English at that time, God breathed on the word "for" as never before and I got a revelation of the word "for" that shook my world! For is a preposition that is used with an object which should be a noun or pronoun. *For* is defined as, ***"Intended to belong to, or be used in connection with; and means 'because' also" (Internet).*** As Pastor Shirley Caesar sings in one of my favorite songs, "Lord, hold my mule!" Hold my mule so I can praise my Jesus, don't stop me, I got to praise my Jesus!! Hallelujah!!! Jesus, Oh my God!!

I connected everything together and I read the scripture with revelation and it meant to me that, "*Because* God so loved *me* that He gave His only begotten Son, that *if I believe* in Him *I would* not perish but have everlasting life. ¹⁷ *Because* God did not send His Son *for* me to condemn *me*, but that *I* through Him might be saved" (*Italics mines*). God changed the nouns to pronouns for me. So now He reveals to my thirsty soul that He sent His Son for me to be saved because HE LOVES ME!!! God loved me! He loved me. God loves me!! God has saved me, but it wasn't until I received the revelation that He loved me and that He loved me "so much" that He gave His Son that I understood and received the 'love of God'!! This revelation changed my life. I could receive His love now.

When you deal with rejection the enemy causes you to believe that you are not worthy of love. So, if you are not worthy of love, you believe that no one can or will love you. The enemy lulls you into believing and accepting that you are unlovable.

That's what he did to me. He made me believe that because of the molestation by my father, his father and my first cousin, being raped twice on the same day, getting pregnant as a result of the rapes, no one would be capable of loving me. I would never be loved by anyone including God. I was so jacked up in my mind, heart and soul; I could not even believe that God could love me. The devil is a liar and a deceiver, hear me, the devil is a liar and the father of lies!

Furthermore, you have to believe that you deserve love; and you deserve to be treated better. Therefore, you won't settle for any crumbs of affection, and you won't fall for guys who talk out the sides of their necks. Also, you will desist in being so desperate for attention and love that you will believe a lie on the spot even though you are saved and filled with the Holy Spirit.

You will surely stop falling into the traps of the enemy by ending up with people who don't deserve an ounce of your time. When you accept physical abuse, emotional abuse, sexually abuse, and mental abuse, you are declaring foolishly that "at least I got somebody". Someone is knocking you upside you head, blackening your eye, withholding affection, love, finances, respect, honor and decent treatment from you and you think it is ok, but you keep telling yourself that "it's not that bad". Let me help you right now. Yes, it is bad!

To get healed, you need to stop lying to yourself right now. If you are in an abusive relationship and you are worth so much more. Again, that's what happened to me. I was so hungry for acceptance and so hungry for love and approval that I married men who couldn't give me what I needed because some were just as damaged as me. You will attract what you are. Because of my relationship with God, I chose to marry men so I would not fall into fornication. I exchanged sex for marriage.

I can admit here that what I wanted was not sex, but companionship where I can get hugs, comfort, support, approval, etc. I didn't care for sex; it was just a means to an end. You have to tell yourself the truth no matter how it hurts so that you can be healed. In order to get my healing and receive God's love I had to admit the truth behind my shame.

Sex was what they wanted and I wanted marriage; so they married me. I used to say all the time, that at least I was married to the men I slept with since I got saved. I married these men for the wrong reasons. I have since asked God to forgive me and I asked three of the men to forgive me. I was so messed up on the inside that I even remarried one of my husbands despite him having had beat me, cheated on me, berated me, and belittled me.

My numerous marriages have caused me great shame, but I was comforted by the fact, that at least I was married. I understand now that I was messed up emotionally and mentally because of the ravages of my past. It's not an excuse; it is just the truth anyhow. The spirit of the deception was in operation and I deceived my own self into thinking that the 'sex act' was love. I have found out that sex doesn't have anything to do with love. Tina Turner should have taught me that through her film, **"What's Love Got to Do with It?"** It's been highly documented that Turner was also in an abusive marriage. Abuse crosses socio-economic lines as well. A person can be wealthy and still be incased in an abusive relationship. God loves you no matter what situation you find yourself. He loved me even when I was being abused.

God loved me and He did not allow them to take my life. For example, my second husband kidnapped me while we were separated and going through a divorce. He took me to a motel and raped me over and over. He beat me, punching me on my body so that I wouldn't have bruises on my face. With his hand, he tried to rip my private part out because he said he did not want another man to touch me. Finally, he went to sleep in a drugged out haze. I slipped out of bed and put on part of my clothes and ran to my car. Once I started the car, he heard me. As I backed out of the parking lot, he stood at the hood of my car and fired his gun five times, but at that moment I had an open vision. I saw a cloud in the shape of a hand come down out the sky and cover my estranged husband's his hand. No bullets were fired. After I pulled out on Stony Island and pulled off, I heard five shots rang out. (This is one of several supernatural experiences I had since I was a child. God has always dealt with me in dreams and visions).

God saved my life because my husband said he was going to kill me so no one else would have me. Another time he tried to kill me in the parking lot at Percy L. Julian High School in Chicago, but my principal, was getting out of his car and stopped him from shooting me. He called him a "yellow belly coward". My principal invited him out the car so he could deal with him. He told him if he ever caught him anywhere near me he was going to have the Chicago Police arrest him and he would go to jail for life and that the guys in the jail loved wife beaters. I thank God for my boss. God used him to help me on a morning when I looked down the barrel of death. I thought my life was over then. But God love me and my principal cared. God's love is a powerful thing. He used my boss to deliver me out of a horrible situation.

Still, the enemy convinced me that I wasn't worthy of life, so I believed that I should do the world a favor and just kill myself! Throughout my life death had been a constant friend to me. The spirit of death lurked in the shadows of my mind. After I refused to let my father rape me, I started running away at night to prevent him from bothering me while my mother was at work. The spirit of death was on me and I would walk in the middle of a dark road until I saw bright lights from cars or trucks approaching; I would just close my eyes praying that they would run over me. The drivers would always swirl around me; sometimes screaming and cursing at me as they passed. Many times I would lie in the ditch praying for snakes to kill me, but they never came.

I was deceived and blinded by the enemy and I couldn't see that God had given me the best reason to live, my son, Victor! One time after receiving a severe beating from my husband, I took a whole bottle of Ibuprofen. The pills came up after a few minutes, I couldn't hold them down. It was God. I felt guilty living since my sister's death. I didn't feel I was worthy of the air I breathed. But when I realized that the enemy comes to "steal, kill, and destroy" I understood that my companion death came from the pit of hell.

The devil had an assignment to kill me so that I would not be here today to help God's people who are yet *"bleeding in the pews."* Jesus gives us hope in His word for He says, **"Come to Me, all you who labor and are heavy laden, and I will give you rest. ²⁹ Take My yoke upon you and learn from Me, for I am gentle and lowly in heart, and you will find rest for your souls. ³⁰ For My yoke is easy and My burden is light" (Matthew 11:28-30).** All we have to do is come to Jesus and give him our burdens and He will exchange them without charge. In Proverbs 10:16, the writer states that, **"The labor of the righteous leads to life, the wages of the wicked to sin.** God says the same in another scripture, **"For the wages of sin is death, but the gift of God is eternal life in Christ Jesus our Lord" (Romans 6:23).** The wisdom that I received through the word of God showed me that even suicide is sin. It is God Who breathes the breath of life into us. The enemy had not been authorized to kill us or to make us kill ourselves. According to **John 10:10**, Apostle John states that, *"The thief does not come except to steal, and to kill, and to destroy. I have come that they may have life, and that they may have it more abundantly."* The devil has his assignment, but Jesus has the ultimate assignment which is to give us an abundantly life in Him!

Through the illumination of God's word, I received the revelation of how much God loved me. The healing came when I believed the words in my Bible as God shined light on them so I could see the depth of His love. Yes, how did God heal me? God healed me through the power of love and deliverance.

DELIVERANCE

What does deliverance mean? Deliverance is what you receive once you have been delivered. According to **Dictionary.com**, deliver is defined as *"to set free or liberate"*. So when God delivers you He delivers you into the realm of deliverance where you have been set free and liberated from all of the enemy traps, schemes, and plans. I accepted God's love and He delivered me. He changed my mindset and then He delivered me! God purged me, He cleansed me, and finally, He delivered me! In the word of God there is a scripture that David wrote when he was in a place of trying and testing that gave me courage and strength. David says to God, ***"Create in me a clean heart, O God, and renew a steadfast spirit within me" (Psalms 51:10).*** I am here today to tell you that God will give you the right desires of your heart when your desires line up with His word and will. It is His will for our lives to have a clean heart with the right spirit in us. How do you get a clean heart and have the right spirit in you? You have to be delivered. How do you get delivered?

First, I had to release all my hurt, pain, past and disappointment to Jesus. Release means to give up, hand over, and to let go. I had to drop it all, but most of all I had to "cast it" to Jesus. The word in 1 Peter 5:7 states that, ***"Casting all your care upon Him, for He cares for you".*** Through His word God taught me to trust His word so I could believe it. Much of me did not think the words in the Bible were for me. When I believed God's word, I was able to cast my cares upon Him. I found out that "the Word works, but you have to work it! This scripture is connected with all the previous scriptures in my book. The enemy clouds our minds to keep us from believing and receiving from the word of God. People of God don't just carry the Bible, but believe the words of the Bible because in them you will find all things that pertain to life.

In December 2005 my Senior Pastor instructed me to launch a Prayer Cell from my home in South Holland. The Prayer Cell would meet every Saturday at noon for one hour. We would have prayer, the Word, Fellowship and Prayer. We were trained to do exactly that. The Man of

God was such a visionary who could see what most of us couldn't see. We begin the Prayer Cell in February with twelve guests. The Prayer Cell grew to fifty people (I had an adult group that I taught and my daughter Minister Ronneisha taught the teens and kids). Our house was overflowing so Apostle Dozier sent me out to look for a place where we could meet. We were able to rent the largest sanctuary at a funeral home on 87th Street in Chicago for a great price.

So, June, 2006 we launched Power & Light West Christian Center in Chicago at Achlin Funeral Home. The church grew to over one hundred and fifty members by 2007. God is so amazing to me. The people that came were like me: wounded, bruised and battered in one way or another. God gave me such a supernatural love for them. If I had held on to unforgiveness and the lack of trust, I would not be capable of God using me to love and facilitate healing in their lives. He sent the hurt, disadvantaged, and broken people to me and God began to do the miraculous in the ministry. This move helped confirm to me that God was delivering and healing me along with the people He was sending into the ministry.

My Senior Pastor was so elated with the work we were doing. He had sent me out along with nine other leaders. Even though, God called me to Pastor in 1995, but I remained in my role as Pastoral Care Elder because I felt I was being a blessing in my position. In 2001 God called me to be an Apostle. I continued to operate where my leader positioned me. So when I was positioned as the EIC (Elder in Charge) of Power & Light West Christian Center, God was still tugging at my heart to Pastor.

In July 2007, my Pastor ordained me as Pastor of Power & Light West Christian Center. God called me out to launch my own ministry in March 2008.

Through God, I launched Love & Deliverance International Ministries in Chicago with twenty-one members. My obedience to God came at a great price. There was a great loss of friendships and relationships that I had for over nearly twenty-three years. But I obeyed what God told me to do. In time He has begun to heal these wounds and reconnect friendships and relationships. Thank you, Jesus! There will always be a great price you pay for obeying God. Obedience costs and its high!

On August 3, 2009, God challenged me in two areas that I had resisted for years. When you get delivered the first thing you have to do is to follow instructions.

On August 3, 2009, I was sitting in a workshop for my job as a CPS high school teacher and the English Department Chairperson, when I heard God speak to me. He said for me to get my things and go out to the sidewalk. His voice was so loud in my spirit I began to look around the crowded room to see if anyone else heard the voice. When I got outside, God told me it was over. God told me that my work as an English teacher was done and He was calling me off my job into full-time ministry.

Immediately I called my then husband and he encouraged me to obey God. I thought about how much money I was making. I was on track to make my highest salary ever which was $140,000.00. I stood on the sidewalk a few minutes. One of my newest teachers came out; I hugged her and said goodbye. She cried. I called and made an appointment for the next day at the Chicago Teacher's Pension Board. During my meeting at the Board, I found that I would earn less than one-third of what I was making. I was asked did I still want to retire. My answer was, "Yes"!

The second area God challenged me in was to accept my calling and have a service confirming me as an Apostle! I had left previous ministry when God called me to launch Love & Deliverance International Ministries a year earlier. That had been a very trying time for me, but God called me out, I obeyed. God always have a ram in the bush. God told me to set a service and to call it an Apostolic Confirmation. He gave me date and the two apostles who had already confirmed that I was called as an Apostle.

So, on September 19, 2009, I was confirmed as an Apostle by Apostle D. A. Richie and Apostle Jenette Taylor at my Love & Deliverance International Ministries in Chicago. My family, church family, and friends were truly supportive and helped push me into my destiny as an end-time Apostle. Thanks to all of them.

On February 10, 2010, I was blessed to receive this encouraging word from one of my international mentors. He told me, "You are indestructible, you are unstoppable, when one door closes, another opens; God is going to spread you beyond familiar territory, get ready...all eyes will see it and glorify God even persecutors of old will see and come to restitute. They will come and bow at your feet." Sometimes, when you are walking in a new level of obedience, you will walk alone. Very few will understand you, but keep walking. Then God will send you a word through another vessel to encourage you.

I thank God for the vessels He sent and even the vessels that the enemy sent. But I had to learn how to obey God to get deliverance. As I obeyed God, He delivered me. God began to deliver me each time I obeyed Him. Because of my obedience, God blessed me to travel nationally and internationally. The lid was removed; that which held me was broken.

The initial supernatural occurrence after God delivered me was when I was ministering in London, England (UK) on January 8, 2011. Standing at the podium, the Lord asked me, "Do you know where you are? I said, "Yes, Lord, London! As I stood at the podium God gave me such a supernatural download. He reminded me of the prophetic word He released to me when I was nine years old when He told me I would preach all over the world. He then began to speak to me again right there and God said: *"Daughter, I called you as a child and I told you that* you would preach all over the world. Look where you are standing. I have called you for such a time as this. . I have taken away the shame and reproach from you. I have healed you from your past. You don't know who you really are but I will tell you, daughter. You are a woman of love, an Apostle of My Love. You will travel and teach my sons and daughter how much they mean to Me. You will teach broken people how to be healed. You will no longer be captive in abusive relationships. Yes, my daughter I am even delivering you now. You will no longer settle for less because I will send you My best. It will not be as in times of old for you. For you are to be treasured and you are to be loved because you are filled with My love, but it will be that a son shall come and he will love you because of His love for me. Let go of that which does fit, but hinders you and you shall see this come to pass. You will know it because you will be loved before you have been seen. By faith, receive what God speaks to you and it shall come to pass not many days hence. Receive it daughter." The word of God says, **"But without faith it is impossible to please Him, for he who comes to God must believe that He is, and that He is a rewarder of those who diligently seek Him"(Hebrews 11:6)**. By faith I was able to receive what God spoke to me. It moved me forward in my deliverance.

Of course, I began to weep because I was amazed at the timing and word of the Lord. I received this word and like Mary, Jesus' mother, I pondered it in my heart. I was just in shock during the rest of the conference where I was confirmed for the second time as an Apostle by

Apostle George Akalonu and the International Ministers Fellowship. Oh, what a mighty God we serve.

As I was sitting quietly weeping after my feet had been washed during the foot washing ceremony. After the Ordination Service, I was shocked to open my eyes to see this gorgeous, tall, and very attractive lady with long flowing red hair kneel at my feet with tears rushing down her face. I didn't know her name then but I saw her during the service. She began to tell me her name and that she was sorry for interrupting me. Apostle Veralyn Kuen shared that she had to come to wash my feet. I let her know that my feet had already been washed. She said, "Please, I need to wash your feet because there is such an anointing of love on your life." She continued, saying, "God is saying that you are an 'Apostle of Love' and you will travel the world and spread God's love and it will cause people to be delivered. I want to wash your feet that I might receive of the anointing of love on your life." I released her to wash my feet. Her tears covered my feet and I experienced such an outpouring of the Love of God as she washed my feet. I was so humbled and blessed by this anointed vessel of God.

The second supernatural occurrence I had after I was delivered was when I traveled to Washington, D.C. for a conference. On February 19, 2011, I stood on the steps of Justice of Supreme Court with a group of world leaders from Africa, London, England, along with my dear friends, Apostle Daf McQuarter and Pastor Lillie Jones and her husband,

and other leaders from the United States, to pray there. Tears rolled down my cheeks as we prayed. I heard God say, *"Look at where you are daughter!"* As I anointed the doors and the statues there, I knew God had sent me as an instrument of deliverance to the nations.

My dear friends, Apostle Fred and Pastor Kathleen Harris, Apostle Stacy Slaughter, Apostle Sondra Jenkins, Apostle Sam and Irene Enyia, Apostle Francis and Prophet Debra Seaton-Chinaka and Prophetess Cleota Porter have been instruments God used to confirm my destiny. God have used them several times to confirm what God has spoken to me concerning my destiny. It is so important to have the right relationships to encourage and pray you through your journey. These powerful men and women have cried with me, prayed for me, and rejoiced with me along the way and I am grateful to the friends God has given me in the four corners of the earth.

Since my London trip, doors have been opened to me in Africa, Italy, Ireland, Germany, and Pakistan. Nations are calling me to come. As Paul was hearing the Macedonia call, I am hearing the call of nations. Pastors in the nations of Africa and Pakistan have called me. These calls did not come until God delivered me and He did it in a way where I knew it without a shadow of doubt. In order to teach and preach love and deliverance, I had to know experientially. Now I am ready for nations.

I knew that all that I had gone through has been for purpose. Not everyone God uses have picture perfect lives. God uses people who have failed, made mistakes, and have run away from God. He uses people who have gone to church all their lives who have a deep love for God, but through no fault of their own have suffered immensely and their lives have been devastated. As such was I, a woman who like the Samaritan woman at the well who had had five husbands and the one she was with was not her husband, but God used her to preach after one encounter with Jesus.

Sometimes, God will use you while you are *"bleeding in the pews"* because He knows the depth of your conviction and pain. God knows how surrendered your heart is. I continually sought after Him in my pain. I drew near to Him and He drew near to me. Though I was bleeding in the pew, I came to understand that it was part of my purpose. I was called by God to those who have been hurt, emotionally, physically and sexually abused, mistreated, rejected, and who live lives in shame and fear. They, too, can be delivered and healed through the power of God's love. God wants them to know that they can be delivered through His love. It's their inheritance.

CHAPTER 10
CONCLUSION

Remaining true to myself, I am sharing in this book what I have never shared before. One of my greatest fears is that if people really knew me they would not like me. I have found that it doesn't matter if everyone doesn't like me. The important thing is that God loves me and I love myself. I am worthy of love, happiness, and peace. God has placed many in my life who love me in spite of my story. They see what God sees when He looks at me; a woman who knows how to love!

My prayer is that those who read this book will be able to seek the healing they need or that many will get clarity about abuse. I pray that leaders will come to understand that there are yet many in our churches who are acting out because they are *"bleeding in the pews"*. We don't know their story; they do.

Please know that Jesus loves you and He cares. If He can pick me up and turn me around, He will do the same for you. God has called us to be the head and not the tail. He has called us to be great people of God. In Jeremiah 29:11, it says, **"For I know the thoughts that I think toward you, says the LORD, thoughts of peace and not of evil, to give you a future and a hope."** God has a plan for us; it is a plan of good and not evil. His plan is stronger than the devil's. All we have to do is believe

God!

God sent His Son to break down the walls that we built to wall others, pain, hurt and disappointments. But the strange thing about walls is they not only wall others out, they wall us in too! Allow Jesus to tear down your man-made walls and let Him reconstruct you into who you have been called to be.

No person defines us. Having children does not define us. Being married or having a relationship cannot define us. Making good money cannot define us either. Only Jesus can define us. There's a scripture that gave me strength to believe God. It states that, **"Therefore, if anyone is in Christ, he is a new creation; old things have passed away; behold, all things have become new" (2 Corinthians 5:17).** Being around Jesus is not as powerful as being in Him. We have to get all the way in Him and surrender and allow Him the authority to work in us the hope of glory.

People of God, we have to actually hand over the controls to Jesus and let Him have control of every area of my life. Once I allowed Jesus into the driver's seat, He drove me in the right direction, toward the right decisions because now I truly learned how to follow directions.

I gave up and let God. In London, God showed me I deserved love and that I deserved better. He bought me out of a loveless marriage, he delivered my husband from a broken woman and gave him a woman who was whole who could love him. He healed my heart, He delivered my soul. I understand since my deliverance that because of the anointing that is on my life, demons have been assigned to me to stop me, to kill me by any means necessary. I understand more clearly that demons have been assigned to stop not only me, but you too. If you are reading this book, then know that demons are plotting even now to rob or strip you of the anointing that God has placed on your life.

My journey to healing lasted from 1996 until 2012, sixteen years. It may take many turns for you, but stay on the journey. Part of the journey is knowing how and when to let go of what is not healthy for you. Sometimes, we hold on to a bad situation because of fear of being alone. That was my final hurdle, fear of being alone. I made the declaration and I decreed that God would deliver me or deliver my husband. A year after returning from London, my husband moved out of my life and it was over. As long as we hold on to what is not working you will never get to what will work. I thank God that my ex-husband and I are friends today.

We have to get rid of strongholds, mindsets, and bondages to be free to be blessed. I found that you have to make room to receive a blessing. God will make room for your gift. He made room in my heart to receive love.

It was not of my making or doing. God did it. I did not construct or pick the time for love this time. I wasn't even looking or thinking about it. My focus was on ministry. On October 20, 2012, I was out to dinner with three of my spiritual children, one was a Prophet. We were thanking God for how He bought me out of a difficult situation. We were praising God when the Prophet looked at me and said, "Apostle, let me know when you want me to start praying for your husband to come. You are going to get married again!" Immediately, I said, "I don't want." And God snatched the words out of my mouth. I just shook my head because I had already had my share of husbands and marriages. As we ate, I thought about this and I resolved to keep moving forward by enjoying life and building the Kingdom of God. Over the next two days I forget what the Prophet said.

God's timing is not like our timing. His thoughts are not like our thoughts. Can these bones live? Can this heart love again? God's word tells us that, **"Do not remember the former things, nor consider the things of old. Behold, I will do a new thing, now it shall spring forth; shall you not know it?" (Isaiah 43:189-19).** God had prepared me for this "new thing" but I didn't see it coming. That's why I know it was all God, and nothing else!

Love knocked on my heart Monday, October 22, 2012. I received an unexpected phone call that changed my life. This call was the beginning of what God meant when He talked about two people becoming one flesh. I have dreamed of love, and have prayed for years that it would happen to me. I had kept my heart open to the possibility of love, but it eluded me. What began as an informative conversation lead to love and a proposal before we ever saw each other. It was a God love that we could not avoid. Love moved into my heart and took up permanent residence.

Pastor Schuyler Vincent Stone knew that God had given him a true treasure in me. He won my heart. Oh, what a beautiful journey of love we shared for fourteen months and nineteen days. What happened? Now you have to read my next book of hope, love, dreams, death, pain, and finally redefining my life as I move forward.

APPENDIX

Boldt, Robert L. *Great Bible Studies.* 2003. (Web). 12 Dec 2013.

"Child Sexual Abuse". *Medline Plus.* U.S. National Library of Medicine. 02 April 2008.

"Cycle". Def. 1-4. *Merriam-Webster Dictionary.* (Web). 10 Oct 2013.

"Effects of Rape on Its Victims". World Health Organization. 2002.

"For" Def. 2. *Dictionary.com.* (Web). 26 Jan 2014

"Healed". Def. 1. *Merriam-Webster Dictionary.* (Web). 20 Mar 2013.

"Hold My Mule". Shirley Caesar. 1989. Song.

Meyers, Joyce. *Beauty for Ashes.* Warner: New York, 1994.

"Myths & Facts About Domestic Violence". The American Medical Association (AMA). (Web). 17 Aug 2014.

"Perversion". Def. 1. *Merriam-Webster Dictionary.* (Web) 10 Oct 2013

"Rejected". Merriam-Webster Dictionary. (Web).

Seamands, David. *Healing for Damaged Emotions.* David C. Cook Publishing: Colorado, 1981

Stronger (What Doesn't Kill You). Kelly Clarkson. RCA. 2012.

U.S. Bureau of Justice Statistics. *2000 Sexual Assault of Young Children as Reported to Law Enforcement.* 2000.

U.S. Department of Health & Human Services, Administration for Children and Families. *1995 Child Maltreatment Survey.* 1995.

U.S. Department of Justice. *National Crime Victimization Survey.* 2008-2012.

"What's Love Got to Do with It". Brian Gibson. Buena Vista Pictures, 1993. Film.

Dr. Phil's Child Sexual Abuse Warning Signs

If you're worried that your child is being sexually abused, look for the following possible warning signs:

- Changes in behavior: withdrawal, fearfulness, crying without provocation
- Night sweats with screaming or shaking, and nightmares
- Regression to more infantile behavior: bedwetting, thumb sucking
- Loss of appetite or other eating problems
- Poorly explained injuries: bruises, rashes, cuts, genital pain or bleeding
- Sudden reluctance to be alone with a certain person
- Unusual interest in or knowledge of sexually related matters; inappropriate expression of affection

"They often won't tell you straight up that something is happening to them, because they've been threatened, they may be ashamed, or they may not want to talk to you about it," Dr. Phil says. "Think about these warning signs and ask questions. Create a dialogue if you're worried about what's going on with a child."

For more information and to learn additional warning signs, visit these websites:

If you believe you need immediate assistance, please call your local emergency number or the mental health crisis hotline listed in your local phone book's government pages.

Because DrPhil.com does not operate, supervise, or exercise any control over any of the therapists, resources or referral services listed, it makes no representations or warranty whatsoever, either expressed or implied, regarding any information or advice provided by these referral services.

In no event shall it, Dr. Phil or the producers of the show be liable to you or anyone else for any decision made or action taken in reliance on information provided by these therapists, resources or referral services.

Childhelp USA's National Child Abuse Hotline
1-800-422-4453
(1-800-4ACHILD)
http://www.childhelp.org/

Rape Abuse & Incest National Network
1-800-656-4673
(1-800-656-HOPE)
http://www.rainn.org/

National Domestic Violence/Abuse Hotline
1-800-799-7233
(1-800-799-SAFE)
1-800-787-3224 TTY
http://www.thehotline.org/

American Academy of Child and Adolescent Psychiatry
www.aacap.org/publications/factsfam/sexabuse.htm

American Psychological Association
http://www.apa.org/topics/sexual-abuse/index.aspx

National Center for Missing and Exploited Children
http://www.missingkids.com/home

Medline Plus
www.nlm.nih.gov/medlineplus/ency/article/007224.htm

ProtectKids
www.protectkids.com/abuse/abusesigns.htm

National Center for Post-Traumatic Stress Disorder
http://www.ptsd.va.gov/index.asp

FindCounseling.com
www.findcounseling.com/journal/child-abuse/sexual-abuse-incest-statistics.html

Stop It Now!
www.stopitnow.com/warnings.html

ChildLuresPrevention.com
http://www.childluresprevention.com/

Corine H. Stone

List of Adult Symptoms of Child Sexual Abuse

Psychological/Behavioral

1. Post-traumatic stress disorder
2. Anxiety disorder, including depression
3. Suicidal tendencies
4. Dissociative behavior
5. Compulsive and irrational sexual habit or behavior
6. Paranoia and distrust towards others
7. Fear of building relationships
8. Eating disorders
9. Sexual dysfunction
10. Drug and alcohol addiction

Physical

1. Insomnia and other forms of sleeping difficulty
2. Obesity or malnourishment due to eating disorders
3. Frequent headaches
4. Chronic back pains
5. Gastrointestinal problems
6. Pelvic pain
7. Respiratory disorders like asthma
8. Musculoskeletal problems

    Unfortunately, for many victims, the trauma they experienced when they were young will not just go away easily, even if they have lived an entire life after it. Adult symptoms will always be there with them. But it doesn't mean that they just acquiesce and allow themselves to be consumed by it. This is why there are so many treatments and therapies out there that seek to help adult survivors of child abuse.

    <u>Child sexual abuse offenders</u> are a top concern for many parents across the nation. It is important to understand that most

abusers are well known acquaintances to their victims. You can find out important stats and tips at Child Refuge.

    We want everyone to understand that a child sexually abused needs to be believed, protected and supported in order for the abuse to stop and healing to start.

Article Source: http://EzineArticles.com/?expert=Cecilio_Calizar

ABOUT THE AUTHOR

Apostle Corine H. Stone is a woman who has experienced much pain in her life. As a child, she was molested for nine years and at fifteen she was raped twice on the same day by two different men. Not only did she have to overcome these devastating events, but she had to endure years of the effects of being molested and raped.

In this timeless book, Apostle Corine shares the process God took her through so that she could be delivered and healed. Her desire is to see others, who have suffered the pain of rape, delivered and healed that they will be launched into their God-given destiny.

Apostle Corine is the Senior Pastor & Overseer of Love & Deliverance International Ministries located in Chicago, Illinois. She has been in ministry for over forty years.

Apostle Corine is a woman that is truly after God's own heart. She is known as "*Mother of Love* and *Mother Apostle*". Apostle Corine was married to the late Pastor Schuyler Stone who went home to be with the Lord June 19, 2014. She has three children: Victor LaShawn Williams (Alicia), Freda Shvonne Hunt and Ronneisha Corine Hunt-Jackson (Sammie). Apostle Corine is the proud grandmother of four grandchildren: Victor II, TeKeia, Jyreh Corine and Sammie, Jr. They are great supporters of the ministry and assignment on Apostle Corine's life.

Apostle Corine lives in the south suburbs of Chicago.

For bookings, speaking engagements, and/or to order books, contact:

Corine Stone Ministries

Apostle Corine H. Stone

P.O. Box 428

Glenwood, Illinois 60425

Phone: (708)314-8675

Email: corinestoneministries@gmail.com

Website: www.corinestoneministries.org

www.ingramcontent.com/pod-product-compliance
Lightning Source LLC
Chambersburg PA
CBHW071709090426
42738CB00009B/1722